KATHERINE MANSFIELD

Katherine Mansfield

CLARE HANSON
and
ANDREW GURR

© Clare Hanson... For information write:
St. Martin's Press, Inc., 175 Fifth Avenue, New York, NY 10010
Printed in Great Britain
First published in the United States of America in 1981

ISBN 0-312-45093-3

Library of Congress Cataloging in Publication Data

Hanson, Clare.
Katherine Mansfield.

1. Mansfield, Katherine, 1888-1923. Criticism and interpretation.
I. Gurr, Andrew, joint author.
II. Title.
PR9639.3.M258Z69 1981 823'.912 80-28131
ISBN 0-312-45093-3

ST. MARTIN'S PRESS NEW YORK

ISBN 0-312-45093-1

Library of Congress Cataloguing in Publication Data

Hanson, Clare.
    Katherine Mansfield.

1. Mansfield, Katherine, 1888-1923—Criticism and interpretation
I. Gurr, Andrew, junior author.
II. Title.
PR9639.3.M258Z69   1981   823'.912   80-24334
ISBN 0-312-45093-1

Contents

Acknowledgements

The authors are grateful to the Alexander Turnbull Library, Wellington, New Zealand, and to Queen's College, London, for allowing access to manuscript and unpublished material.

Acknowledgement is also made to the Society of Authors and to the Estate of Katherine Mansfield for permission to quote from material still in copyright.

1 Introduction

The myths

Katherine Mansfield was born in October 1888 in Wellington, New Zealand. Her baptismal name was Kathleen Mansfield Beauchamp. In the early stages of her career as a writer she used names and pseudonyms, some of them variants of her baptismal name, some complete inventions, though for her serious work she found and kept the name Katherine Mansfield from quite early on. She tried out other names and roles too. In March 1909 she married George Bowden, but left her husband the morning after the marriage. In May 1918 she became Mrs John Middleton Murry, in a kind of converse of her first marriage — she had been living as Murry's wife since 1912, and remained with him except for intervals prompted by her poor health until her death in the Gurdjieff Institute near Paris in January 1923.

The names, including the marital names, which she was given or took for herself reflect in various ways the pressures under which a woman living in England in the early years of the century and who was powerfully impelled to make herself 'free' was likely to be put. She adopted, deliberately or not, a wide variety of roles with which she tried to explore the paths of freedom. She enjoyed inventing nicknames for herself and for most of the people drawn into her various acts. Her fiction shows the same determination to impose her own shape on the often intractable realities of her life. Names from her childhood regularly appear, often only slightly adjusted, in her stories. The central figure of several early stories set in New Zealand is called 'Kass', her family's name for her. Later it was altered to Kezia, the child-observer of the major New Zealand stories. Names of real people and places, Stanley, Maata, Karori, were deployed in only slightly altered circumstances. Other names, when used directly, were adjusted minimally: Beauchamp became 'Beetham', and later

'Fairfield'; Waters became 'Trout'; Tinakori Road became 'Tyrell Street'. The initial impulse to free herself from given names, given roles, was followed by the creation in her fiction of delicately adjusted revisions. The adjustments were her assertion of the subjective nature of vision and memory, and the imitations produced some of the finest short fiction written in English.

Her life and her fiction were tightly interlocked. She became, in fact, better known as a personality than as a writer, a perspective which is still with us today, since most criticism of her writing has a strongly biographical slant. There are dangers in this perspective, because her personality was many-sided, and few of her contemporaries saw exactly the same side. None can have seen her in the round. As her close friend Ida Baker put it,

> She was like a lantern with many windows — not octagonal, but centagonal. Each friend had his or her window and K. gave generously, gave all to each one, of her light, through that window. That was why so many people thought they were, not just one of her friends, but her only friend. She did not give the lantern, and no one could touch the flame — and if anything came too close she would withdraw or close her leaves.[1]

To see the flame clearly, without the distortions of any one window, we need to look at her writing rather than the myths of her life. But before reaching the central task, it is worth looking at the kinds of myth which she fostered, and then at some of the realities in which the myths took root.

In effect there were two kinds of myth about Katherine Mansfield, the witch and the saint. To D. H. Lawrence especially she was a destructive, witch-like figure, ultimately apotheosised, if that can be the word, as Gudrun in *Women in Love*. Katherine Mansfield was an independent and forceful woman, with a caustic wit very well calculated to find out Lawrence's weaker points. So, in *Women in Love*, he counter-attacked in his presentation of the destructive personality and sexuality of Gudrun Brangwen. And in characterising Gudrun's art as a 'miniature' art, he not only makes a slighting reference to Katherine Mansfield's chosen story form, but also hits back at what he insisted on seeing as the purely reductive quality of her mocking and sardonic wit.

The contrary perspective of her as a saint was created very largely by her husband and literary executor, John Middleton Murry. He assiduously filleted and rearranged her notebooks for publication after her death, making sure they conformed with his personal idea of her. Their relationship was an essential feature of the last decade of her life. He came close to claiming it as the only feature. In essence he saw her as a genius who was forced by the pressures of social insecurity to become aggressive, bitter, attitudinising, bitchy and satirical, with the manner characterised in her writing by *In a German Pension*. As their relationship developed through the last years of her life, according to Murry, she turned away from her bitter attitudinising to her proper self, which primarily involved the expression of the kind of love found in the stories set in the New Zealand of her childhood. Murry gave prominence to her own identification of this change, which once led her to identify as separate impulses what she called her 'two kick-offs in the writing game',[2] and he went so far as to date it from the time when she was reunited with her young brother Leslie before he died in France in 1915.

Murry's myth of a Katherine Mansfield whose cast of mind gradually changed under the influence of their loving relationship from satirical and bitter to joyful and loving is not borne out by the evidence, except for some of the letters in her correspondence with Murry which he published in 1951. To some extent the love expressed in those letters was another of her roles, another act for the distraction of the outside world. It would be more realistic to see her development through that last decade in terms of a withdrawal, first into the 'world of two'[3] which she set up with Murry, and subsequently, even before the tuberculosis which turned so much of the last period of her life into the reclusive existence of an invalid, a retreat into the total privacy of her own vision of her childhood world. That world she shared only with her dead brother. For a time she consciously cast Murry in the role of surrogate brother, but in the last years she rejected even that, as she was able to forgo the last comfortable illusion of a brother-companion in her by now wholly private world.

Murry's influence on writers of biography and criticism of Katherine Mansfield has been extensive and, largely because he controlled the materials relating to her life and work, often difficult to identify. A lot has been done in the last twenty or so years to adjust Murry's perspective, but sometimes the effect has been merely to replace one myth by another. Leonard Woolf, for instance, returned to the witch myth, though without Lawrence's malignity, in order to correct Murry's version. He saw Murry's influence on her as destructive, and voiced his preference for her witch personality as the one closest to the real Katherine Mansfield. She could make him laugh, he wrote, more than anyone he had ever known. 'Her gifts were those of an intense realist, with a superb sense of ironic humour and fundamental cynicism. She got enmeshed in the sticky sentimentality of Murry and wrote against the grain of her own nature.'[4] Woolf's view puts the woman who satirised the bourgeois first, and consequently highlights in her best work such relatively minor elements as the complacent materialism of Stanley Burnell or the equally complacent feeling of captivity of Jonathan Trout in 'At the Bay', at the expense of most of the elements which make her later work so distinctive.

Katherine Mansfield was neither a saint nor a witch, but a complex and forceful person whose adoption of different masks and roles at different times confused and bewildered even her nearest observers. In a sense, her role-playing was a deliberate strategy. She wished to keep her real self hidden and private. Her 'real self' she always thought of as that of an artist. It is ironic that the defensive myths which she herself helped to create should have obscured the art that was all she really cared about.

Some realities

She was born in a colony which was always conscious of its existence as a dependency, a cultural transplant, cut off from the faraway metropolis. She was brought up in a suburban setting aware of but separated from the city centre. For three years in adolescence she found the cultural capital of her world, when she was sent to London with her older sisters to complete her schooling at an academy in Harley Street. She went back with her family to New Zealand determined to be a writer, to make her mark in the metropolis, and within two years she had gained the freedom to do so. She returned to London in 1908, shortly before her twentieth birthday, and plunged into the business of sampling life which she thought was the primary prerequisite for creating art. In the next four years she had several love affairs and many transient jobs. A miscarriage in a forlorn village in Bavaria, an abortion and her one-day marriage were among the consequences of the love affairs. Acting, including dancing in a chorus line in Liverpool and working in several casual jobs for which she felt qualified by her early training for a musical career, were amongst her other experiences. Her father gave her a regular allowance, but she never had enough to feel truly free, and her sole ambition, to write, demanded more free time than her allowance readily permitted.

As a writer she had published short pieces in periodicals since before leaving New Zealand. Poems, stories and articles appeared spasmodically through the years from 1909 to 1912. In February 1910 she began an association with A. R. Orage's *The New Age* and its coterie of writers and journalists that lasted for more than two years, her first durable involvement with the literary metropolis. Orage's coffee-shop editorial meetings gave her an audience and therefore a purpose and shape for her work. Her role-playing, her talent as an entertainer in person and on paper, now had a reasonably substantial identifiable audience. She wrote sharp, satirical pieces, literary parodies, feminist polemic (Orage's companion and co-editor was Beatrice Hastings, a South African nine years older than Katherine, an ardent feminist and a potent influence), and, most substantial, the stories which appeared in *The New Age* as 'Bavarian Sketches', the basis for her first book of stories, *In A German Pension*.

There are many accounts of her life at this period, by friends as diverse as Beatrice Campbell and Lawrence. One slight anecdote not noted by her recent biographers is in a letter from Edward Marsh to Rupert Brooke. It has the mixture of verbal precision and muted glee that was a characteristic note in the letters of the literati of the time, but the plausibility of the anecdote still stands out through the mannerisms of the writer. 'Katherine Tiger', wrote Marsh, using Gilbert Cannan's nickname for her,

> got turned out of an omnibus the other day for calling a woman a whore. She really ought to remember she's a Lidy. The provocation was that the woman said that all suffragettes ought to be trampled to death by horses. Katherine tho' not a suffragette protested, and the woman said, 'You with your painted lips!' Rather a squalid little story.[5]

In the wake of Emily Davison's death under the King's horse during the 1913 Derby feelings did run high. But the extremes of language, and Marsh's implication that under the skin she was more a colonial than a lady, fairly capture her situation in London at this period. She was too vulnerable. In the end she turned for refuge to a single, stable relationship with a man who shared her priorities and who could give her the access to publication she still needed, the editor of *Rhythm*, the second major outlet for her writing, John Middleton Murry (1889–1957). Murry was still at Oxford when they met, but full of literary ambition. In the years of their association he established himself as a successful literary journalist and critic.

They made a team, the two tigers of the literary world, writing and editing together until their publisher, who had also produced *In a German Pension*, decamped and left them with a massive debt. She had to pledge the allowance from her father; Murry became a bankrupt. The financial and social pressures on the two of them proved as severe as they had been on one. In the first five years of their association they had at least twenty-one changes of address. Financially, socially and in literature they were on the outskirts, members of what Virginia Woolf acidly termed 'the underworld'. Two of the changes of address linked them with Lawrence and Frieda, in an association which gave Lawrence some of the material for *Women in Love*, but it was not a fertile link for either Katherine Mansfield or Murry. Until 1916 she was casting around, experimenting in style and subject, with little consistent success apart from the 'Bavarian Sketches' for

The New Age. It was a formative but not a fruitful period.

The arrival of her brother Leslie (also known as 'Chummie' or 'Bogey') in February 1915 to join the war, triggered a number of changes. First he lent his sister enough money for a trip to France. It was basically a romantic escape from Murry's cool self-control into a torrid encounter with Francis Carco. She later put the three of them into the triangular relationships of 'Je ne parle pas français'. The Carco affair got something out of her system, and when she returned to Murry she began writing *The Aloe*, the first of her major New Zealand stories, stimulated by her talks with Leslie and developing a length and strength she had never been able to sustain before. (She tried composing a novel several times, but always abandoned it. The nearest she came to achieving it was in the finished New Zealand stories of her greatest creative period, 1920-22, which were to have been built into a novel called *Karori*, the suburb of Wellington in which the Burnell family of the stories lived.)

Then in September 1915 Leslie was killed in a training accident in France. She responded to the news with an intense hysteria which was aggravated by the joy she had found in evoking the brother-and-sister memories of Karori, and also by the ill-health which had been sapping her physique and making her increasingly febrile for the past two years. Escape was vital. Murry took her to Bandol in the south of France in November. He returned to London in December but rejoined her in January. The three months which followed, January to March 1916, were in Murry's eyes the high point of their alliance. They spent each day sitting opposite each other writing. *The Aloe* began to be reshaped into *Prelude* in those months, and the essentials of the form in which the best of the stories are composed were established then. Murry became for a time a kind of surrogate little brother (she even called him 'Bogey', or 'Dark Bogey' to differentiate him from fair-haired Leslie, and referred to the two of them as babes in the wood, lost children together). For the time of the 'Bandol idyll' he acted the part she cast him in, of companion into the recesses of her childhood memories.

It was not a role which could be sustained for long. However escapist her own role-playing was, she was too much the cynical realist that Leonard Woolf found in her to play that game beyond reason. They returned to England in April for another attempt at a link with the Lawrences, and then for the next eighteen months drifted on indecisively, still on the literary outskirts, still attitudinising. In the autumn of 1916 she performed the feat in defence of Lawrence at the Cafe Royal which Lawrence gave to Gudrun in *Women in Love*, sweeping out of the café clutching Lawrence's writings which were being ridiculed by some acquaintances. She started writing again for *The New Age*, without telling Murry. In January 1917 they set up separate establishments, with the kind of semi-detached relationship described in 'Psychology'. *Prelude* was given to the Woolfs in 1917, as one of the first Hogarth Press publications. The other books which launched the Hogarth imprint were by T. S. Eliot, E. M. Forster, Virginia Woolf and Middleton Murry.

Then in October 1917 both she and Murry suffered renewed attacks of the pleurisy which had first attacked them in April 1914. Once again she had to escape the English winter by journeying to the south of France. This time, however, the place of the earlier idyll had been turned by the war into a place of nightmare. Murry was too committed by his war work in London to join her, an ordering of his priorities which she did not forgive. The situation was fraught and depressing, and she was exhausted in mind and body. Then in February she began to spit blood, and was diagnosed as tubercular. At this point her devoted friend from school days, Ida Baker, arrived in Bandol, having persuaded hostile authorities to let her through wartime France. Ida Baker played a unique role in Katherine Mansfield's life, which she has described herself in her book *Katherine Mansfield: The Memories of L.M.* ('L.M.' being one of her nicknames). During the early years of the alliance with Murry, Ida kept in the background, and went out to Rhodesia for some years. After the second Bandol period she became an indispensable companion, though she could not replace Murry.

Katherine Mansfield now felt simultaneously isolated from Murry, spiritually and physically, and more than ever closely bound into dependence on him. By a further well-wrought irony her long-awaited divorce from George Bowden was now coming through. So after three traumatic months in Bandol she set off back to London, accompanied by Ida Baker, to the chill brand of security which Murry offered her.

They did marry, in May 1918, though it had taken three miserable and exhausting weeks of struggle through war-disrupted Paris to get back to England, and she took a long time recovering from the mental and physical strain. Once again she tried to survive a winter in England, married and living in Hampstead, her husband with a secure income from his editing, herself with a regular outlet for her work in her husband's journal, now *The Athenaeum*. But for all that it was not a productive time. She never wrote at her best in England. Some of her finest creative periods, in Bandol in 1916 and in Switzerland in 1922, were when Murry was beside her. But in England she was self-conscious, uneasy. Her best work was composed in a clear, open atmosphere where she could feel free. Paradoxically, the constraints put on her by her disease and which forced her out of England gave her exactly that freedom.

For the winter of 1919–20 it was once again necessary to go south. She went with Ida and Murry to Italy. Again Murry could not stay with her, and again she felt abandoned. San Remo proved nearly as painful as the second period in Bandol had been, and at Christmas Murry arrived to give her what support he could. On his departure she once again collapsed, physically and spiritually, and was rescued by an elderly relative and her companion, whom she had met when her father visited her in San Remo, and was taken to stay in their villa in Menton. She returned to London for the summer of 1920, but went back to Menton in September, to a villa of her own, with Ida. By this time she knew her situation with fearful clarity. Murry offered her physical aid and security, but spiritually her rejection of him was almost complete. He was a companion like Ida, no more. She hated the fact that she needed him as much as she hated Ida's anxious motherliness. But her disease left her no option. Above all, she was terrified that death was imminent, and began an increasingly frantic search for increasingly unlikely cures. These circumstances ruled the last two years of her life. She retreated, spiritually, deeper and deeper inside herself and her private memories, where she was unaccompanied and utterly free. She moved restlessly from place to place seeking a cure for the fate she knew she shared with Keats and Chekhov. And she wrote with power and intensity her greatest, most concentrated stories.

By 1920 money had ceased to be a constraint on freedom. *Bliss, and Other Stories* was published by Constable in December 1920, *The Garden Party, and Other Stories* in February 1922. Murry, although he gave up his editorship in 1921 to live with her in the Swiss Alps where she was trying to hold off her tuberculosis, also had a reasonable income. They were established, reputable, even famous. Through the two summers of 1921 and 1922 she wrote incessantly, creating enough stories to make up two further collections, which Murry was to publish in 1923 and 1924 after her death. Not until August 1922 did she give up what she finally acknowledged was a race against time. She made her will and returned to London. Then in October she joined the Gurdjieff Institute near Paris in a last desperately unrealistic attempt to find a cure, an unorthodox regime which she survived (part of the treatment involved sleeping in a loft over the Institute's cows) for three months, until 9 January 1923. Murry arrived at the Institute, of which he thoroughly disapproved, a few hours before she died.

Feminism and the making of an artist

Katherine Mansfield's achievement in making her family accept her as an artist was considerable. She was born in the 1880s into a community whose values were out of date by the standards of late Victorian England, and she was born into a bourgeois family whose greatest ambition for a daughter was that she should marry well. Apart from a distant cousin, there was no intellectual or artistic precedent for her in her home background, as there was for George Eliot or Virginia Woolf. However, she was lucky in her stay at Queen's College, and there was a strong vein of tolerance in her parents which prevented their ridiculing her when she returned to New Zealand full of her artistic ambitions, and which contributed to their decision, extraordinary for its time, to let her return to London to test these ambitions.

Her first model for the artistic personality was Oscar Wilde.

The doctrine, which he propounded in *Dorian Gray* and tried to illustrate in his life, that one could develop oneself into a self-chosen image, that one could literally become whatever one wished, had a decisive influence on her. It was a strategy that could work. She wrote about this in her journal as late as 1921:

> . . . So do we all begin by acting and the nearer we are to what we would be the more perfect our *disguise*. Finally there comes the moment when *we are no longer acting*: it may even catch us by surprise. We may look in amazement at our no longer borrowed plumage.[6]

This suggests one of the means by which she managed to make herself into something far removed from what her home background would have dictated. The Symbolist belief in the artist's ability to create himself, to *become* his mask, sustained her throughout her career.

She also took from Wilde's dramatic enactment of the 'artist life' the sense that although on the one hand experience was a necessary prerequisite for art, on the other hand it could threaten artistic creativity if it were uncontrolled. This was something that she also discovered rapidly through her own experiences in the years between 1908 and her meeting with Murry in late 1911.

Her earliest short stories, written around 1907–8, show a strong sense of conflict between an adolescent desire to play out the conventional feminine role in life (which her mother did) and the desire to be an artist. In 'The Education of Audrey' and 'In a Café', the heroines alternate between a romantic dream of being worshipped by a protective, albeit artistic, male; and the desire to be a successful artist in their own right. The two courses of action are quite clearly seen as incompatible.

Her experiences between 1908 and 1912 deepened her sense of the difficulties attendant on being a woman and an artist. She no longer felt conflict between romantic fantasies and her ambition, but felt instead weakened and humiliated by the failure of her attempts to live as a 'free' woman. At about this time she first began to write for *The New Age*, and it was thus that she came into contact with Beatrice Hastings. Beatrice Hastings's

particular interest was in the plight of married women. Her
argument was that though 'No taxation without representation'
was an irresistible argument for the vote, this would still leave the
majority of women, who were not earning, in the same position
of domestic slavery and sexual exploitation in which they had
been for centuries. She called for a 'real feminist league' which
would rouse all women to an awareness of their position. She
wrote a series of articles for *The New Age* on these questions, and
also wrote stories which invariably depict the loss of energy and
vitality in an articulate woman who marries and has children —
reflecting her belief that motherhood, especially, was incompatible
with intellectual and moral freedom.

This was obviously calculated to appeal to Katherine Mansfield,
coming at exactly the time, after her return from Bavaria, when
she was most sensitive to the idea of her biological nature as a
trap. Though Beatrice Hastings's ideas may have been exaggerated,
it was through her that Katherine Mansfield first came into
contact with feminism as a genuine force, and through her that
she was able to place her personal sense of conflict in a wider
context. Under Beatrice Hastings's influence, she wrote several
articles and stories for *The New Age* on feminist themes: for
example, the uncollected 'At the Club', 'A Marriage of Passion',
and 'The Mating of Gwendolen'. Many of her 'Bavarian Sketches'
in *The New Age*, later published in *In a German Pension*, deal
with the same issues: for instance, 'At Lehmann's' and 'Frau
Brechenmacher Attends a Wedding'. In these stories she explores
the economic factors that may force women into marriage against
their will, and also the widespread ignorance of sexual matters
that led to so much stress and disillusion for women. Through her
writing she thus relates her own rejection of the conventional
married role to a wider historical and social background, and in so
doing justifies her position, and her efforts towards freedom.

When she met Murry, her difficulties as a woman and an artist
were eased enormously. Not only was Murry distinctly non-
aggressive, but he had the great virtue of being able to recognise
Katherine's talent, and to acknowledge that it was greater than
his own. There is a great deal of evidence for this — indeed, her
own letters make it clear — but as just one example of Murry's

insight, one might quote this diary entry of his, written sometime in 1917, when she was working on *Prelude*:

> Tonight Katherine read me three 'Spring Pictures', which she wrote in France in the spring of 1915, when she was in the flat on the Quai aux Fleurs. They are such stuff as only she can do . . . Katherine, when she is Katherine, writes like the South-West Wind. The world is moist, calm, urgent under its touch. All colours have a new life . . . Thus she reveals the secret life, not merely of minds (which I may sometimes do) — not merely of men and women (which again even I *might* do) — but of the whole vast world.[7]

But in her early struggle to become an artist, she felt the need to liberate herself from her weak position as a woman quite as strongly as she felt the impulse to flee from her bourgeois home. The dual nature of her struggle to become an artist is neatly exemplified in two sets of quotations copied into her early notebooks. In the 1954 *Journal* Murry printed all the aphorisms from Wilde urging the artist to self-development and rejection of convention. He omitted, however, almost all of an equally large number of quotations from *Daniel Deronda*. This was the book in which George Eliot explored more openly than in any of her other books the pressures on the woman-artist. The figure of the Princess, Daniel's mother, who has rejected the maternal relationship in favour of her art, was still clearly relevant in 1908 when Katherine Mansfield was beginning to write:

> 'No', said the Princess, shaking her head and folding her arms with an air of decision. 'You are not a woman. You may try — but you can never imagine what it is to have a man's force of genius in you, and yet to suffer the slavery of being a girl. To have a pattern cut out — [8]

After 1912 she wrote no more overtly feminist stories like those for *The New Age*, though some feminist polemic appears in *The Aloe*, carefully pruned away when the story was refashioned into *Prelude* in 1917. Yet there is what must be called a feminist awareness running throughout her writing, in the sense that there is always a strong feeling of division and discontinuity between male and female experiences of life. As in the fiction of Virginia Woolf, male and female roles are polarised, and only rarely does the experience of the two sexes meet and become communicable — as for example in the scene between Linda Burnell and the 'weak' male, Jonathan Trout, in 'At the Bay'.

New Zealand and exile

As a writer Katherine Mansfield produced no single magnum opus. Consequently there is no obvious focus for assessing her achievement or even for identifying her distinctive qualities. Readers who follow Leonard Woolf's preferences will take *In a German Pension* as her most characteristic achievement, and rank the other stories accordingly. The childhood stories will seem stickily sentimental, products of a maudlin escapism. Readers who find her social analysis, particularly of the oppressed position of women, to be her most conspicuously acute and illuminating feature will similarly range the stories according to a preference for which there is a good deal of supporting evidence but which still provides only a limited perspective on the whole achievement. And the view which takes the New Zealand stories, especially *Prelude* and the other stories written for the *Karori* collection, as most characteristic will also be limited in so far as it draws attention away from the distinctive qualities of the stories set in Bavaria or London or France. It is difficult to find a central organising principle for assessing her achievement that does not lead to neglect of some aspect of her work. She shines out through too many lantern-faces for any single perspective to give an adequate view. The best we can do is identify the different perspectives, and which face they lead up to. Of them all, probably the broadest is the one relating her exile to the powerful evocation of New Zealand in the major stories of her last years.

The last seven years of her life, the years of her mature achievements from *Prelude* onwards, were years of retreat into an isolation made perfect only inside the private circle of the childhood world that she constructed with such meticulous precision. She continued to use Murry and Ida Baker for physical protection, but in her stories she went where neither could hope to follow. She had written work based on her relationship with Murry — 'Je ne parle pas français', 'The Man without a Temperament', 'Psychology' — but all of them were in some degree part of the dialogue which they maintained throughout their lives together. As such they perhaps lack the complete detachment and freedom, which writing out of more distant recollections provided.

Rather more than half the stories in her total *oeuvre* are based on or set in New Zealand. Murry's version of her outlook — that she hated the closed-off complacency of bourgeois suburban New Zealand until Leslie's death, when, as she put it, 'quite suddenly her hatred turned to love' — is a thorough oversimplification. She was trying out a narrative by 'Kass' about two little 'Beetham' girls early in 1910 ('Mary', published in *The Idler*, March 1910. 'Kass' also appears in 'The Little Girl' of 1912). 'A Birthday', set amongst the Bavarian stories of *In a German Pension*, has a New Zealand setting. The story which first drew Murry's attention, 'The Woman at the Store', written towards the end of 1911, was based on her memory of the camping holiday she underwent (over 240 miles on horseback) in the Ureweras shortly before she finally left New Zealand in 1908. And two stories written in 1915 before she began *The Aloe* have distinct affinities with the later New Zealand material. 'The Apple Tree', first published in *The Signature* in October 1915 under the title 'Autumn I', is a gently derisive anecdote about her father, told from the viewpoint of his children, girl and boy. 'The Wind Blows', published as 'Autumn II' in *The Signature*, is a more oblique piece about brother and sister, poignant, discontinuous, foreshadowing the symbolist technique which evolved as *The Aloe* changed in the following years to *Prelude*. Both stories were presumably triggered by the reminiscences of their childhood that she was sharing with Leslie at the time. His death, which took place just before the two stories appeared, changed the tentative, exploratory impulse into a powerful compulsion. From then on she drove towards the ultimate goal of a complete evocation of Karori in a series of minutely detailed epiphanies.

Prelude showed her that her New Zealand background was the best quarry for her artistic materials. It contained so much of the experience which, up to that time, she had most deeply lived. Only such experience could be the proper food for her art. This realisation is recorded in a famous journal entry of 1916:

> I feel no longer concerned with the same appearance of things. The people who lived or whom I wished to bring into my stories don't interest me any more. The plots of my stories leave me perfectly cold. Granted that these people exist and all the differences, complexities and resolutions are true to them — why should *I* write about them? They are not near me. All the false threats that bound me to them are cut away quite.
>
> Now — now I want to write recollections of my own country. Yes, I want to write about my own country till I simply exhaust my store . . .
>
> Ah, the people — the people we loved there — of them, too, I want to write. Another 'debt of love'. Oh, I want for one moment to make our undiscovered country leap into the eyes of the Old World. It must be mysterious, as though floating. It must take the breath. It must be 'one of those islands . . .'[9]

From this point on, when she began to see her New Zealand background as an artistic positive, something which would both nourish her as an artist and enable her to express something wholly individual, she gained enormously in confidence as a writer.

There is no doubt that she worked at her highest creative level on material that was removed from her in space and time. This is because she was a Symbolist writer, interested not in social contexts and realities, but in the imaginative discovery or recreation of the ideal hidden within the real. With the aid of distance in time and space it is the idealising imagination, or perhaps more precisely what Pater would call 'the finer sort of memory',*

* which sees its object 'with a great clearness yet . . . raised a little above itself, and above ordinary retrospect' (Walter Pater, 'The Child in the House', *Miscellaneous Studies,* Macmillan Library Edition of the Works of Walter Pater (1910), p. 172).

which can best discover the ideal essence of experience, which is obscured in the confusion of immediate impressions and perceptions.

The short story form

Katherine Mansfield and Rudyard Kidpling are among the very few writers in English to establish a reputation entirely on the basis of the short story form. It is no accident that they were writing at approximately the same time. The development of the short story in England lagged behind that in America and Russia chiefly because of differences in opportunities for magazine publication. By the 1890s, however, a huge expansion in the numbers of quarterlies and weeklies created the situation described by H. G. Wells:

> The 'nineties was a good and stimulating period for a short story writer . . . No short story of the slightest distinction went for long unrecognised . . . Short stories broke out everywhere.[10]

Two entirely different types of story flourished together at the close of the nineteenth century. First, there was the story with a definite plot, which was the lineal descendant of the Gothic tale; and second, there was the new, 'plotless' story, concentrating on inner mood and impression rather than on external event. The latter was associated especially with *The Yellow Book*, the famous 'little magazine' of the nineties, and with the circle of writers gathered round its publisher John Lane — George Egerton, Ella D'Arcy, Evelyn Sharp and others. The innovatory quality of many of the stories published by these writers, and the contribution that they made to the development of the short story, is now becoming increasingly evident.

The plotless story seems to arise naturally from the intellectual climate of its time. In a world where, as the German philosopher Nietzsche declared, God was dead, and evolutionary theory had produced a sharp sense of man's insignificance in a changing universe, the only alternative seemed to be the retreat within, to the compensating powers of the imagination. With such a retreat came the stress on the significant moment, which would be called 'vision' or 'epiphany' by later writers such as James Joyce — the moment of insight which is outside space and time, vouchsafed only fleetingly to the imagination, but redeeming man's existence in time.

In fiction a shift in time-scale seems to accompany this emphasis on the moment. Throughout the nineteenth century the unit of fiction had been the year — from *Emma* to *The Ambassadors* we can say that this was so. In the late nineteenth and early twentieth century, the unit of fiction became the day. Elizabeth Bowen has written of this, saying that Katherine Mansfield was the first writer to see in the short story 'the ideal reflector of the day'. It is perhaps significant, however, that many other writers began their careers with short story writing in this period – Forster, for example, with the aptly named *The Eternal Moment*, and also D. H. Lawrence, James Joyce, and Virginia Woolf. It can even be suggested that the novels of these writers — Lawrence excepted — are in a sense simply extended short stories. Virginia Woolf's *Mrs Dalloway* is an obvious example, but there is also Joyce's *Ulysses*, originally projected as a story for his collection of stories called *Dubliners*, to be titled 'Mr Hunter's Day'. It is as though the short story is the paradigmatic form of the early twentieth century, best able to express its fragmented and fragmentary sensibility.

Katherine Mansfield certainly saw her kind of story as a quintessentially modern form, a point she makes more than once in her reviews of fiction for *The Athenaeum*. She was also very conscious in her use of epiphany as the focal point of her stories. In one of her reviews she discusses the way in which internal crisis has replaced external crisis of plot in modern fiction, at the same time warning against the loss of all sense of crisis or significance which she detected in the work of some modern novelists:

Without [the sense of crisis] how are we to appreciate the importance of one 'spiritual event' rather than another? What is to prevent each being unrelated — complete in itself — if the gradual unfolding in growing, gaining light is not to be followed by one blazing moment?[11]

It is usual in discussing Katherine Mansfield as a story writer to emphasise the influence of Chekhov on her technique. The relationship between her fiction and the plotless story of the nineties, however, is probably more important. She modelled her early stories on those of the *Yellow Book* writers, and it is from them, not Chekhov, that she would have learnt the techniques of stylised interior monologue, flashback and daydream which became so important in her work. By 1909, which was when she probably first read Chekhov, his techniques must have seemed distinctly old-fashioned by comparison with much English fiction.

Chekhov was probably more interesting to her as a type of the artist, especially after she contracted the tuberculosis from which he also suffered, rather than being a specific influence on her work. The two writers differ fundamentally in that Chekhov is a far more realistic writer than Katherine Mansfield. His characters are always rooted firmly in a social context, and social forces are shown to have a decisive influence on the course of their lives and feelings. The difference is best shown by a comparison of his story 'Sleepy' with Katherine Mansfield's version of it, 'The-Child-Who-Was-Tired' (1909). Chekhov's story is a restrained, pathological study, in which action is convincingly related to a specific social and psychological context. Katherine Mansfield's story is a symbolic fable, in which certain elements of the original plot are exaggerated and key images repeated in order to express a general, rather than a specific truth: the harshness of woman's lot in life. Although she read and admired Chekhov's stories throughout her career, a limit must be set on any comparison between the two writers. Any easy identification of the two is misleading.

Katherine Mansfield's talents were peculiarly suited to the short story form, as, in a different way, were those of Kipling. She did, however, try on at least three occasions to write a novel. There is the early attempt, *Juliet* (1906); then a novel to be based on the life and experiences of a schoolfriend she had known both

in London and New Zealand, *Maata* (written intermittently
between 1908 and 1915); finally the novel, *Karori*, which was to
be built around the *Prelude* and 'At the Bay' material, and to be
based on the Burnell family. She was planning this last novel as
late as 1921—22. Speculation about what she might or might not
have written is futile, but clearly she continually wanted to
experiment with new forms and to widen the boundaries of her
talent. Another way of getting out of the critical rut of seeing her
solely as a master of the concentrated short story is to recognise
the clear development in her later work towards the use of the
story cycle form. Two distinct cycles emerge: that centering on
the Burnell family (*Prelude* — 'At the Bay' — 'The Doll's
House') and that centering on the Sheridans ('The Garden Party'
— 'Her First Ball' — 'By Moonlight' — 'The Sheridans').
Although they are all New Zealand stories, the two cycles are
quite separate, and are clearly associated in Katherine Mansfield's
mind with different themes. Broadly speaking, the Burnell
sequence is concerned with the difficulties of the child or young
adult coming to terms with the brutal realities of life (the egotism
and cruelty of other people, the pressures of sexuality and so on),
whereas in the Sheridan sequence there is a much more elegiac
note: the theme is, as Katherine once wrote of Hardy's poems,

> that love and regret touched so lightly — that autumn tone,
> that feeling that 'Beauty passes though rare, rare it be . . .'[12]

The fact that the two sequences were quite distinct is clear from
a journal note written as Katherine Mansfield was planning 'The
Sheridans':

> I must begin writing for Clement Shorter today [this refers to
> a contract she had with *The Sphere*] 12 'spasms' of 2,000
> words each. I thought of the Burnells, but no, I don't think so.
> Much better, the Sheridans, the three girls and the brother and
> the Father and Mother and so on . . .
>   And in that playing chapter what I want to stress chiefly is:
> Which is the real life — that or this? — late afternoon —

these thoughts — the garden — the beauty — how all things
pass — and how the end seems to come so soon.[13]

The stories in the Sheridan and Burnell cycles are linked together
by character, setting and theme, and by repeated images and
motifs. A 'dynamic pattern of recurrent development' is established, so that the reader's experience of an individual story is
enriched by and enriches his experience of the others in that
sequence.

Katherine Mansfield did not herself separate the short story
and novel form as absolutely as genre-conscious modern critics
have done, and the cycle of related stories may be seen as a kind
of bridge for her between the two forms — rather as in William
Faulkner's *Go Down Moses*, or, more relevantly, in Joyce's
Dubliners, a sequence of stories linked together loosely but firmly
by a common setting, related characters and related themes.
Joyce similarly employs the symbolist technique of imagery
repeated throughout the stories.

Symbolism

The relationship between Symbolism and Katherine Mansfield's
short story art has been insufficiently recognised. It is accepted
that her contemporary, Joyce, was influenced decisively by his
early contact with Symbolist literature, but Katherine Mansfield's
critics and biographers have failed to register the similar
influences at work in her case. They have dismissed her early
writing in the Symbolist mode as immature and, by implication,
irrelevant, not seeing the intimate connection between this
early work and the particular nature and scope of her achievement.

The main influence on her in the period up to 1908 when she
left New Zealand for the last time was that of Arthur Symons,
who also influenced so many other early twentieth-century
writers, notably Yeats and Eliot. Symons's role was as a
communicator and purveyor of ideas. It was through his critical
books[14] that Katherine Mansfield was introduced to French
Symbolist poetry and to other diverse, broadly Symbolist writers

like the Belgian Maurice Maeterlinck and the Italian Gabriele D'Annunzio. She also absorbed very thoroughly the condensed version of Symbolist aesthetic theory which Symons presented in his books. Indeed, her early attempts to piece together an aesthetic rely almost entirely on the writings of Symons, and to a lesser extent Wilde. From these two, she took ideas which continually influenced her art. One was the Symbolist belief that in literature an abstract state of mind or feeling should be conveyed not through descriptive analysis but through concrete images or symbols. Such a theme must be evoked, not described, if it is to be successfully conveyed in art. If we read her stories in the light of this ideal — one which she refers to repeatedly in letters and notebooks — it becomes apparent that in a Mansfield story almost every detail has a symbolic as well as a narrative function. The details, or images, are intended to work in concert to create a mood or evoke a theme which is never directly stated. These oblique and indirect stories must thus be read with the same close responsiveness as a Symbolist or Modernist poem, if the full effect is to be realised.

She was also influenced by the Symbolist belief in the organic unity of the perfect work of art. Even in her earliest stories she strove to achieve the 'unity of impression' advocated by Poe, and she wrote many years later that 'If a thing has really come off it seems to me there mustn't be one single word out of place, or one word that could be taken out.' This particular quotation might tend to suggest that she was concerned only with a super-ficial perfection of style, but her other references to the 'essential form' of the true work of art make it clear that for her such form was truly organic, uniting form and content indissolubly.

Though the work of art could be considered as analogous to natural organic life, it was also, paradoxically, outside organic life, outside reality. She certainly inherited the Symbolist belief in art as an autotelic activity, a fact which should be stressed as a corrective to the impression, frequently given by critics, that she was a writer with a 'mission' or purpose. In fact she was clear in her belief that, though art must be nourished by life, it had its own laws and nature, which were quite distinct from those of reality. The artist must be completely aware of the distinction, and must not confuse the two spheres, nor attempt to impose his vision on life:

> That is to say, reality cannot become the ideal, the dream; and it is not the business of the artist to grind an axe, to try to impose his vision of life upon the existing world. Art is not an attempt of the artist to reconcile existence with his vision; it is an attempt to create his own world *in* this world.[15]

From Symbolist theory and practice came her interest in extending the boundaries of prose expression. Baudelaire and Mallarmé in their prose poem experiments were interested in steering prose away from its innate structural tendency towards abstraction and analysis, towards a more concrete expressiveness. They and other Symbolist writers — including Pater — attempted to convey meaning in prose not only through the use of words as conceptual counters, but also by exploiting the 'physical properties' of language, and 'sound sense'. They repeatedly used the musical analogy for prose, to signify an ideal of non-discursive expressiveness, and this is an image which is also used by Katherine Mansfield, for the same reasons, in her frequent discussions of what she was trying to do with her prose medium. For example, she wrote of 'Miss Brill':

> After I'd written it I read it aloud — numbers of times — just as one would *play over* a musical composition — trying to get it nearer and nearer to the expression of Miss Brill — until it fitted her.[16]

Towards the stories

Criticism of Katherine Mansfield's work has tended to fall into four distinct categories: biographical criticism, interpreting the stories in the light of the known events of her life; studies seeking to isolate the special quality of her writing, often using such terms as 'delicacy' and 'sensibility'; 'influence' studies, in this case dealing almost exclusively with the influence of Chekhov on

Katherine Mansfield; and 'objective' critical studies which appeared in large numbers in the heyday of the New Criticism, when the short story was a favoured subject for close textual analysis. More recently, under the influence of structuralist theory, there have been analyses of Katherine Mansfield's stories in terms of their narrative structure and technique.[17] The main problem is that most early criticism was done under the shadow of Murry's highly selective presentation and publication of his wife's writings. In the fifties and sixties there was a noticeable slackening of interest, and it is only recently that there has been a renewed interest combined with more well-informed criticism.

The stories first appeared in five separate collections: *In a German Pension* (1911); *Bliss* (1920); *The Garden-Party* (1922); *The Doves' Nest* (1923); and *Something Childish* (1924). These were brought together in 1945 as *The Collected Stories of Katherine Mansfield* — which has never been out of print since, but which is in fact incomplete. A fair number of stories which appeared in magazines like *The New Age* and *Rhythm*, for example, were never traced and reprinted. As far as the New Zealand material is concerned, however, Ian Gordon's *Undiscovered Country* (1974) brings together almost all the stories, including previously uncollected ones such as 'Old Tar', and also the unfinished ones first printed either in whole or in part by Murry in the *Journal* and *Scrapbook*.

Katherine Mansfield's reputation is of a writer with an exquisite and delicate sensibility. Her writing is most often described as though it were a kind of verbal equivalent of an Impressionist painting, and stress is laid on the physical 'surface' of her work — its tone, colour and texture. She is commonly praised for her acuteness of ear, her visual memory, her exquisite rendering of impressions of the natural world. There is a string of verbal nouns — flash, colour, sparkle, glow — by means of which her critics have tried to convey the effect that her work has had on them. But it can more usefully and accurately be compared to Post-Impressionist rather than to Impressionist painting, for we need more emphasis on the solidity of the structure of her stories and on their weight of implication. In this

Cézanne, whom she admired, is a better parallel than Renoir, whom she did not.

The depth of her themes and the technical awareness of her art will best emerge in discussion of individual stories. In the chapters which follow, the emphasis will accordingly be on the evolution and development of her work, with the minimum of further biographical detail.

2 The early work up to *Prelude*

Katherine Mansfield first began to write at about the age of fifteen, and her first pieces to be published, in the *Queen's College Magazine*, are precociously sophisticated, despite the fact that at this time she did not yet see herself as a writer. Until the time she left Queen's College, she was convinced that her vocation lay in music, attracted perhaps by the glamour of the musician's way of life, and also following the example of Arnold Trowell, the young 'cellist whom she had met (and idolised) at home in New Zealand and again in London.

After her return to New Zealand in 1906, she decided in favour of a literary rather than a musical career and from this point on she practised and experimented with her writing tirelessly, adopting the craftsman-like approach to her art which remained with her throughout her life. The style of this early writing is diverse and reflects the range of influences on her — her models included figures as disparate as her cousin 'Elizabeth', author of the popular novel *Elizabeth and her German Garden*, Oscar Wilde, the Brothers Grimm, and George Bernard Shaw.

But despite this diversity of influence, the early work falls into two main categories. First there are the 'child' stories, mainly anecdotal pieces evoking her own childhood world, but bathed in a cosy and reassuring light — for example, 'One Day' and 'Your Birthday' (*Queen's College Magazine*, December 1904, June 1905). There are, however, other 'child' stories with fantastic or fairy-tale elements which show the other side of *Prelude's* garden. In these stories children are vulnerable victim figures most often separated from the adults who should protect them. They face isolation, danger, even death, which is frequently imaged as drowning or falling (for example, in 'His Ideal' and 'Misunderstood').[1] Not one of this second type of story was submitted for publication, but they represent something which is part of the totality of the 'childhood' world of the later stories, shot through as it is with underlying fears and anxieties.

The second major strand in her early work is Symbolism. The larger part of her early writing consists of imitative pieces in the Symbolist manner, with a vocabulary and subject matter drawn from Symons, Pater and Wilde. The form is most often that of the 'vignette' or prose poem pioneered by Baudelaire and Mallarmé and later taken over by Wilde and other writers of the 1890s in England.

Through her vignettes she was able to explore the possibilities of prose as a medium, experimenting with rhythm, cadence and isocolon[2] in a style in which the influence of Pater is especially marked. The structure of the vignettes resembles that of a Symbolist poem: the effect is rather like reading a poem of Verlaine's in prose translation. There is only the most nominal narrative framework, the main focus being on a series of images introduced through techniques of daydream or reverie. These images cohere and combine to evoke a particular mood, subjective emotion and external scene being fused with varying degrees of skill. For example, this section of 'Vignette III' (published in *The Native Companion*, 1 October 1907) evokes rather self-consciously a mood of ennui and claustrophobia. The vocabulary and prose rhythms are distinctly Paterian (indeed, later in this particular vignette there is a direct reference to Pater's essay on Leonardo).

So I have drawn the curtains across my windows, and the light is intensely fascinating. A perpetual twilight broods here. The atmosphere is heavy with morbid charm. Strange, as I sit here quiet, alone, how each possession of mine — the calendar gleaming whitely on the wall, each picture, each book, my 'cello case, the very furniture — seems to stir into life. The Velasquez Venus moves on her couch ever so slightly; across the face of Manon a strange smile flickers for an instant, and is gone, my rocking chair is full of patient resignation, my 'cello case is wrapt in profound thought. Beside me a little bowl of mignonette is piercingly sweet, and a cluster of scarlet geraniums is hot with colour.

Sometimes through the measured sound of the rain comes the long, hopeless note of a foghorn far out at sea. And then all life seems but a crying out drearily, and a groping to and fro in a foolish aimless darkness. Sometimes — it seems like miles away — I hear the sound of a door downstairs opening and shutting.[3]

Her earliest and relatively uncalculated writing thus veers between the two poles of anecdote and symbolism.

Her first serious attempts at publication, in the Australian journal *The Native Companion* in late 1907, show symbolism gaining the upper hand. The pieces which she submitted for publication, destroying much other material in the process,[4] were all in the Symbolist mode — the prose poems titled 'Vignettes', 'Silhouettes', and 'In the Botanical Gardens',[5] and the story 'In a Café' in the style of *The Yellow Book*. Another prose poem, 'Death of a Rose', was published in *The Triad* (Dunedin) in July 1908. These early publications were a turning point for her, confirming her commitment as a writer and clarifying the direction which her art would take. From this point on, her anecdotal writing was never more than a means of storing impressions, the raw material for her symbolist art.

The first short story she published, 'In a Café', was one of a series modelled on the 'psychological sketch' of the 1890s. The other stories of this kind that she published were 'The Education of Audrey' and 'The Tiredness of Rosabel', both written around 1908, though there are other examples of the genre in the notebooks of this period. Usually the psychological sketch of the nineties was structured around a single scene, flashback and daydream being used to extend the narrative where necessary. This was because the emphasis of the story was on 'mood', a key term for the nineties, and not on external event. Katherine Mansfield's stories concentrate similarly on mood and inner feeling, and follow the basic framework of the psychological sketch. She uses a fairly standard formula in showing a change of inner feeling brought about by an apparently trivial external event — for example, the dropping of a bunch of violets in 'In a Café'. Her use of the techniques of flashback and daydream is rather more distinctive. She used retrospect and dream even in these early stories, not merely in order to introduce extra narrative information, but also in order to establish parallels and contrasts in themes, as, for example, in showing the discrepancy between the 'real' Rosabel and Rosabel seen as a social object in 'The Tiredness of Rosabel'.[6] The thematic patterns are reinforced by patterns of imagery, which are heavily emphasised. Her achievement was in a sense to infuse the symbolist structure of the vignettes into the form of the psychological sketch. In so doing she established many of the essentials of her later method.

'The Tiredness of Rosabel' is the earliest of her stories to have a place in the collected edition of her work. The theme is one to which she returned in a 1922 story, 'A Cup of Tea', turning on the rich girl/poor girl contrast and sexual rivalry. The story is conducted almost entirely through what can most accurately be termed indirect representation of inner consciousness. She does not use interior monologue proper, a direct transcription of a character's thought processes, or even the illusion of it. Her 'interior monologue' is indirect, stylised, filtered through third person, past tense, syntactically conventional narration. The technique seems to have been taken directly from the psychological sketch — it does not appear in the work of other writers whom she was reading at the time, nor in the work of Chekhov, whom she first read in 1909. It was a method pioneered in England by the women writers of the nineties like 'George Egerton' who were anxious to stress subjectivity — the subjectivity of women's experience — and it is perhaps for this reason that it appealed to her. The technique is used successfully in 'Rosabel' to introduce us rapidly to Rosabel's psychology:

> As she swung onto the step of the Atlas bus, grabbed her skirt with one hand and clung to the railing with the other, Rosabel thought she would have sacrificed her soul for a good dinner.[7]

The story operates on three time levels, each having its own psychological dimension. The source of the story lies in the remembered past, in the incident in the millinery shop where Rosabel works and where she encounters the 'rich girl' who is her alter ego. The time level of the present corresponds with the reality of Rosabel's everyday existence — her dingy lodging-house room and the poverty which grates on her at every turn. The time level of the future is one that only exists in dream. Rosabel projects herself, by the aid of the imagination which she possesses in too great abundance for her station in life, into the fleetingly glimpsed *vie de luxe* of the customer. The story is thus constructed around a basic contrast between the shop girl and the débutante, but there are also parallelisms which give the story a further dimension of irony — and which lift it above the level of other early work. Rosabel and the rich girl are not utterly opposed. They are linked firstly because the girl's fiancé, Harry, is also attracted to Rosabel, and makes some crude advances to her. Secondly, it is Rosabel who models the 'special' hat which the customer eventually buys.[8] The hat suits Rosabel equally well; indeed it is said to 'suit her beautifully'. In appearance (one kind of reality) the two girls are equal: in that other reality, measured by the constraints of Rosabel's poverty, they are worlds apart.

Structural contrast and parallelism are reinforced in 'The Tiredness of Rosabel' by a strong pattern of imagery. For example, the image of violets is used repeatedly as an emblem of youthful romantic expectation. Rosabel's first action in the story is to buy herself a bunch of violets, purchased at the expense of 'a good dinner' (food in this story is associated with the reality of sexual relationship, as yet only sensed by Rosabel). Later, in her daydream, the violets reappear, but this time in profusion — 'Harry bought the great sprays of Parma violets, filled her hands with them' — sharpening our sense of the discrepancy between Rosabel's experience and her longings. And as Rosabel goes deeper into her dream, the violets reappear, poignant, overwhelming, seeming to 'drench the air with their sweetness'.

This kind of symbolic design occurs in a more sophisticated, and more unobtrusive, form in Katherine Mansfield's later stories. But the foundations of her method were laid in this early type of 'psychological sketch', and for all their imitative nineties settings and props, it is here that we must look for the origins of her 'unique' method in the short story. The period between her arrival in London in 1908 and her meeting with Murry in 1911 was in many ways the most unsettled of her life, and it is also the least well documented. Her confident impulse to write waned during the time of her affair with Garnet Trowell in the winter of 1908, her one-day marriage of March 1909, and then her subsequent retreat to Bavaria in the summer of 1909, where she gave birth to her stillborn child. It was in the wake of all this, in the late autumn of 1909, that she began her second concentrated burst of creative writing.

This was the work that formed the basis for her first collection of stories, *In a German Pension*. The brittle and satirical tone of these German sketches has usually been attributed to the wretched circumstances of her life at this time, but the literary precedent of her cousin 'Elizabeth' may also have been a factor.[19] The popular novel series which began with *Elizabeth and her German Garden* must have seemed to mirror very exactly Katherine Mansfield's circumstances. The books are set in Germany, and the narrator is an estranged English gentlewoman of sensibility, whose efforts to accommodate herself to the boorishness of German life form the basis for the ironic comedy of the stories.

Isolated and abandoned as the young Katherine Mansfield must have felt in Bavaria, it seems likely that she would have been drawn to her cousin's satirical tales of German life, and would have been stimulated to try and emulate their tone and stance. The impulse may also have been strengthened by her awareness of the social successes which had accompanied 'Elizabeth's' rise to literary fame, for she had gained entrée into a social world far above that of the other Beauchamps.

There is considerable confusion about the dating of the heterogeneous group of stories published first in *The New Age* under the name 'Bavarian Sketches' and then as a book called *In a German Pension*. It seems likely that many of the stories were first sketched out in Bavaria, and some even completed, but that most underwent considerable revision under the guiding hand of Beatrice Hastings before they were published in *The New Age*. The first few pieces to appear (in February 1910) were probably unrevised. These are the ones that show most clearly the influence of 'Elizabeth' — 'The Luft Bad', 'The Baron' and 'Germans at Meat'. The pieces which show more signs of revision are the more substantial feminist stories, 'At Lehmann's' and 'Frau Brechenmacher Attends a Wedding', published later on in the period of her association with the magazine. However, the odd-one-out in the whole group is undoubtedly her famous version of Chekhov's story 'Sleepy', 'The-Child-Who-Was-Tired' (*The New Age*, 24 February 1910).

This story illuminates very precisely the relationship between Katherine Mansfield's art and that of Chekhov. She was probably first introduced to his writing in 1909, in Bavaria, and almost certainly read him initially in a German translation. There can be no doubt that the basic plot of 'The Child' was suggested by Chekhov's 'Sleepy' (1888). In Chekhov's story, a maid of all work is driven crazy by lack of sleep, has hallucinations in which she confuses past and present, and unable to reason any longer smothers the baby she is supposed to nurse. In Katherine Mansfield's story, a young maid is worn out by hard work, falls into daydreams, similarly longs to sleep, and seeing the baby that she has to nurse as the enemy preventing her from this sleep, smothers the child. The events are very close indeed to one another. Yet there are wide differences in texture and emphasis between the two stories that are more illuminating than the narrative similarities. They show that Katherine Mansfield did not absorb Chekhov's manner and approach in the same way in which she had earlier absorbed that of Pater and Wilde.

Despite its violent ending, Chekhov's 'Sleepy' is essentially a realistic story dealing with problems of contemporary life. Through the maid Varka's hallucinations, we are given a substantial amount of information about her past life, her social situation, and the events which have brought her to her present position, such as the death of her father and her having to beg for alms. It is made clear that Varka's life is being ruined by her poverty and by external social forces which are completely outside her control:

Varka sees again the muddy road, the men with satchels, Pelageya and father Yefim. She remembers, she recognises them all, but in her semi-slumber she cannot understand the force which binds her, hard and fast, and crushes her, and ruins her life.[10]

In Katherine Mansfield's story the same basic situation is handled and interpreted very differently. The origin of the child-maid is not the same — her situation is explained simply by the fact that she is illegitimate, which is a symbolic rather than a social fact. It is used to support the theme of revulsion from sexuality and childbirth which is a strong undercurrent in this story, linking it with later feminist stories for *The New Age*. This theme is emphasised in other ways too. The Frau who employs the child is given four children, not one, as in Chekhov, and another is expected. A conversation between gossips is included which has no parallel in Chekhov, and which details the horrors of childbirth at length. At the close of the story it is made clear that the murder of the baby is attributable mainly to the child's despair at being imprisoned with the Frau, her husband, and their endless babies (the claustrophobic smallness of the house is also emphasised):

> 'I don't believe the Holy Mary could keep him quiet,' she murmured. 'Did Jesus cry like this when he was little? If I was not so tired perhaps I could do it; but the baby just knows that I want to go to sleep. And there is going to be another one.' She flung the baby on the bed, and stood looking at him with terror.

'The-Child-Who-Was-Tired' is more inward than 'Sleepy', less concerned with external and social forces. It gives almost all the emphasis to the child's inner feelings, especially her revulsion from the Frau and the babies. It is also less detached. The narrator of the story is involved with the child, and often enters her thought patterns, as in 'Rosabel'. In structure, 'The-Child-Who-Was-Tired' is thus closely related to 'Rosabel' and the other psychological sketches, and it is in this respect that it differs most markedly from Chekhov. Though Chekhov's story contains a central symbol — that of the green light which is associated with death — it remains, like the rest of his work, essentially realistic and metonymic[11] in its narrative progression. Katherine Mansfield's story is to a far greater degree structured according to perceptions of metaphoric similarity or contrast. The contrast between the vulnerable, sensitive child, for example, and her gross, insensitive employers is stressed throughout the story by repeated references to their size and weight, and her fragility and smallness. In its strong thematic patterning, Katherine Mansfield's story is to a much greater degree than Chekhov's a symbolist composition. As in the stories of Joyce's *Dubliners*, the movement forward of the narrative is 'retarded' or subverted by the introduction of symbolist techniques of parallelism and leitmotif.[12] This is true of all the other major *German Pension* stories — for example, 'Frau Brechenmacher Attends a Wedding' and 'A Birthday' — a point that needs some emphasis, as this is a period of Katherine Mansfield's career which is often described as one of realism.[13] Only in the first *New Age* sketches like 'The Luft Bad' does she veer towards anecdote and naturalism. All the longer stories employ techniques that are essentially symbolist.

Her art can be clearly differentiated from that of Chekhov. It is of a later age, when writers were consciously trying to steer prose fiction away from realism, borrowing the techniques of poetry. Chekhov is in many ways one of the less important of the many influences of her early years.

The feminist elements of 'The-Child-Who-Was-Tired' appealed strongly to Beatrice Hastings, and not only 'At Lehmann's' and 'Frau Brechenmacher' (published in *In a German Pension*) but also other more explicitly feminist stories were written for her, notably 'A Marriage of Passion' and 'The Mating of Gwendolen'.[14] Both these stories deal with the theme of marriage as a financial and sexual transaction which is both degrading and restricting for women. With 'A Marriage of Passion' in the same issue of *The New Age* she included a sketch, 'At the Club'[15] in which the same issues were debated in dialogue form.

By the time these later stories were actually published, her association with *The New Age* was effectively over. In March

1912 a story of hers appeared in *Rhythm*, a prototypical twentieth-century 'little magazine' which had just been launched by John Middleton Murry. She had met Murry in December 1911, and by Easter 1912 was installed as assistant editor of *Rhythm*, moving into the centre of his literary as well as his personal life. For both of them, *Rhythm* became the sign and symbol of their artistic ambitions, and despite perpetual financial difficulties, they went on struggling to keep the magazine afloat over a period of two years. Katherine Mansfield was a less regular contributor to *Rhythm* than she had been to *The New Age* but what she did contribute was of a higher quality; and in *Rhythm* she was more closely involved with a genuine artistic community. *The New Age* started as a Fabian–Socialist weekly, and its interest in the arts was always overshadowed by its interest in social, political and philosophical matters. In contrast, *Rhythm* was devoted exclusively, even aggressively, to the arts, and through a combination of luck and Murry's unflagging editorial zeal managed to keep in closer touch with new developments in the arts than many of the more established journals. The magazine's two great enthusiasms were for Post-Impressionism and Fauvism in the visual arts and for 'Bergsonism' in philosophy. Though the work of the French philosopher Henri Bergson is little known or regarded today, it had an enormous influence on artists in the first few years of the century, partly because his stress on intuitive rather than intellectual modes of knowledge gave back to the artist something of his lost status as seer and prophet. Bergon's philosophy was interpreted with considerably more accuracy by Murry than by his 'anti-humanistic'[16] counterpart T. E. Hulme in *The New Age*.

Katherine Mansfield's involvement with *Rhythm* had a distinct and readily identifiable impact on her work. We have her own evidence that she had been impressed by the first Post-Impressionist exhibition, coming in a letter of December 1921 to Dorothy Brett:

Wasn't that Van Gogh shown at the Goupil ten years ago? Yellow flowers, brimming with sun, in a pot? I wonder if it is the same. That picture seemed to reveal something that I

hadn't realised before I saw it. It lived with me afterwards. It
still does. That and another of a sea-captain in a flat cap.
They taught me something about writing, which was queer, a
kind of freedom — or rather, a shaking free.[17]

This letter has been often quoted, but little analysed. What
precisely was the effect Post-Impressionism had on her? Joseph
Frank has argued influentially[18] that one of the characteristics
of Modernist literature as a whole was its preoccupation with
'spatial form', with novelists in particular striving to achieve an
effect of stasis and simultaneity and to short-circuit the sense
of process that is at the heart of their medium. Ultimately,
however, the analogy between the novel and the visual arts must
break down: the one is unavoidably a temporal, the other a
spatial art. But the parallel between a painting and a short story
is closer. The short story takes place over a relatively short period
of time, and can therefore more readily be grasped as an aesthetic
whole. Its spatial and structural elements can be exploited for
aesthetic effect in ways not possible over the longer time course
of a novel.

It is therefore possible to conceive of a genuinely productive
link between a movement like Post-Impressionism and the work
of a young story writer. Katherine Mansfield's own comment,
speaking of 'a kind of freedom — or rather, a shaking free',
points straight to Expressionism as the quality of art which
affected her most. Both Post-Impressionist and Fauve painters
were Expressionist, working in reaction against the realism and
attention to social and external detail of the Impressionists. The
concern of painters such as Van Gogh, and later Henri Matisse,
was to express inner feeling, by means of forms that they felt
need no longer be tied to naturalistic representation. A
characteristic quotation is this one from Van Gogh, taken from
an article on his letters published in *Rhythm*:

> In my opinion Millet and Lhermitte are the true painters of
> the day, because they do not paint things as they are, drily
> analysing them and observing them directly — but render
> them as they feel them . . . What I aim at above all is power-
> ful expression.[19]

Hence the distortion of the naturalistic picture surface which, combined with the use of colour for emotive rather than naturalistic effect, gave rise to the very term 'Fauve'. However, despite this emphasis on emotion and instinctive expression, Post-Impressionist and Fauve art was more rigorously composed and constructed than that of the Impressionists. 'Rhythm', with its suggestion of a musical analogy, was the term most frequently employed by the artists themselves to denote the organic structure which should inform a painting or sculpture. Hence the title of Murry's magazine.

Several stories Katherine Mansfield wrote after 1910 show the influence of Post-Impressionism in their new freedom both of subject matter and treatment. 'The Woman at the Store' is the first example, and may even have been written especially for *Rhythm*, with its Post-Impressionist and Bergsonian ideals.[20] 'The Woman at the Store', 'Ole Underwood' and 'Millie' (published in *Rhythm* and *The Blue Review*) and 'Old Tar' (published in New Zealand only) are attempts to explore those aspects of Katherine Mansfield's New Zealand background which were least acceptable, and accessible, to a London audience. They deal with mental and physical extremes: all four examine pathological states of mind, which are linked with New Zealand as it was experienced by settlers who failed to do what her own parents and grandparents did, which was to establish themselves financially. The stories thus explore a life from which she was exempt, and of which she had glimpses only, for example during the camping journey that she made in the interior of North Island in 1907. Many commentators have suggested that these stories represent a direction which her work could have taken, that she could have been a 'regional' writer, and she has been criticised for not following this path. The stories themselves, however, represent her recognition that she could not be a New Zealand writer in this sense. 'Her' New Zealand was not New Zealand: she had been cushioned from raw contact with the country and its problems, which she could only explore by means of an effort of imaginative sympathy. It is for this reason perhaps that, as Ian Gordon has suggested, the 'regional' stories are not completely successful, always remaining 'at one remove'.[21] But 'The Woman at the

Store' was acceptable to Murry as editor of *Rhythm* precisely because of its exotic, far-away quality. Around the time of the Post-Impressionist exhibition came a growth of interest in primitive and exotic cultures of all kinds, and this prevailing taste among the avant-garde may have been a precondition for the writing of such a story at all.

'The Woman' is often described as a thriller, a story with a plot, but this is not really adequate as a description. Like all Katherine Mansfield's stories, it is concerned primarily with mood or atmosphere, and its events happen outside the boundaries of the story itself. The 'drama' is in fact conveyed wordlessly, diagrammatically, by means of a child's drawing, a device which seems itself emblematic of the oblique narrative technique:

> 'I done the one she told me she'd shoot me if I did. Don't care! Don't care!'
>
> The kid had drawn the picture of the woman shooting at a man with a rook rifle and then digging a hole to bury him in.
>
> She jumped off the counter and squirmed about on the floor biting her nails.

Throughout the story landscape and background are exploited to convey mood. The opening paragraph is a fair example. The description of the countryside mirrors both the exhaustion of the travellers and the desolation of the woman at whose store they must pass the night. The overwhelming heat, the dust, the horse's open sore, the thick spider webs over the manuka bushes, evoke a feeling of depletion, degeneration and corruption. Later, the description of the woman's house and the store itself is used to identify her inner state. The prevailing atmosphere is one of lassitude and neglect, but there is also evidence of other days and other aspirations, and there are repeated suggestions of dislocation between the woman's present state and her potential (for example, in the overstocked, over-ambitious store). Background description, character and feeling merge and realistic description gives way to expressionistic distortion as the climax approaches:

It was sunset. There is no twilight in our New Zealand days, but a curious half-hour when everything appears grotesque — it frightens — as though the savage spirit of the country walked abroad and sneered at what it saw. Sitting alone in the hideous room I grew afraid. The woman next door was a long time finding that stuff.

The story begins abruptly ('All that day the heat was terrible') and ends as casually ('A bend in the road and the whole place disappeared'). Between these two points nothing happens: something is shown. The revelation will have no consequences, for the travellers are too sympathetic to the woman, too initiated into the landscape, to have any ideas of bringing her to justice. In this sense 'The Woman' is not a conventional story; nor is it tightly plotted in the conventional 'thriller' sense. There are longueurs (passages of the story which are apparently without action: crucial to mood, not plot), and then abrupt narrative transitions and omission of expected narrative detail. Yet the story is strongly constructed, as all critics have noted, and the sense of structure comes mainly from the use of leitmotif and prolepsis, which give the story a rhythmical structure analogous to that of a Post-Impressionist painting. An example of leitmotif is the use of the colour red, with its obviously bloody overtones, and also its suggestion of frenzy, taken up again in 'Ole Underwood'. The major use of prolepsis is in the preparation for the revelation of the drawing. There are several near-revelations — the woman's first appearance, carrying a rifle:

As I looked a woman came out, followed by a child and a sheepdog — the woman carrying what appeared to be a black stick. She made gestures at us.

or the child's other drawings, suggesting corruption and disorder:

And those drawings of hers were extraordinary and repulsively vulgar. The creations of a lunatic with a lunatic's cleverness. There was no doubt about it, the kid's mind was diseased.

'The Woman at the Store' is thus the study of an interaction between a character and an environment. Part of the trouble that has driven the woman to murder and the child to near idiocy is the desperate scrubbiness of the surrounding landscape with its pumice dust and mile after mile of tussock grass — but their trouble is also bound up with their domestic situation. The woman was originally a barmaid, 'as pretty as a wax doll'. Taken when she married from a coast town to the isolated store, her life was tolerable only as long as the coach called 'once a fortnight'. After this stopped, her husband started to disappear, leaving her alone to look after the store for long periods. The isolation and his indifference drove her to the violation that is at the heart of the story:

> 'Now listen to me,' shouted the woman, banging her fist on the table. 'It's six years since I was married, and four miscarriages. I says to 'im, I says, what do you think I'm doin' up 'ere? If you was back at the Coast I'd 'ave you lynched for child murder. Over and over I tells 'im — you're broken my spirit and spoiled my looks, and wot for — that's what I'm driving at . . .
>
> 'Trouble with me is,' she leaned across the table, 'he left me too much alone. When the coach stopped coming, sometimes he'd go away days, sometimes he'd go away weeks.'

The feminist element in 'The Woman at the Store' links it with other *New Age* stories of the period, and it is this, combined with its attention to social setting and detail, which produces a degree of confusion and diffuseness of effect not found in the later 'Ole Underwood', where attention is focussed more exclusively on the psychology of the central character.

'Ole Underwood' is dedicated to Anne Estelle Rice, a Fauvist painter and contributor to *Rhythm* who was illustrating Katherine Mansfield's stories at this time. It is the most successful of the expressionist stories, and the most inward. The story is based on a local 'character' from her early Wellington years, and the setting is recognisably Wellington, down to the 'mad wind' which always portends psychological crisis in her work:

The pine trees roared like waves in their topmost branches, their stems creaked like the timber of ships; in the windy air flew the white manuka flower. 'Ah-k' shouted Ole Underwood, shaking his umbrella at the wind bearing down upon him, beating him, half strangling him with his black cape. 'Ah-k' shouted the wind a hundred times as loud, and filled his mouth and nostrils with dust.

In this opening paragraph of the story, the wildness and disorder of the landscape reflects Ole Underwood's mental turmoil. We see the landscape as if through his fractured vision. The extremity of language also suggests his heightened, unnatural sensitivity to external stimuli, with collocated words such as smoulder, roared, snapped, beating and strangling.

Ole Underwood spends his time wandering around aimlessly. Children scatter at his approach; adults avoid him. His history is given laconically by a bystander in a bar:

'Cracked!' said one of the men. 'When he was a young fellow, thirty years ago, a man 'ere done in 'is woman, and 'e foun' out an' killed 'er. Got twenty years in quod up on the 'ill. Came out cracked.'

On this particular day, however, his continual agitation, never stilled since his period in prison, builds up to fever pitch. The intensification of inner feeling is suggested, as before, through externals — background detail is distorted and heightened, as in the opening of the story, for expressionistic purpose. The repetition of gibberish or near-gibberish words also foreshadows the loss of rationality which will occur at the close of the story — 'Ah-k! Ah-k!' from Ole Underwood himself, 'Ya-Ya! Ya-Ya!' from the Chinamen, and so on. The use of colour to reflect mood reaches a peak here, developing from simple oppositions as between Ole Underwood's black attire and the innocent white flowers in the passage quoted above to the complex, all-pervasive use of the colour red. This runs throughout the story, denoting not merely bloodshed and approaching violence, but also suggesting the feeling of agitation, even dread, which makes the blood pound in Ole Underwood's head, which makes him crush the red flowers in the bar, and which finally makes him ignore the threat of the prison hanging over the town with its 'red walls'. Colouring of red and black is interwoven through the story until the climax, which comes just after he has 'looked once back at the town, at the prison perched like a red bird, at the black webby clouds trailing'. At this point he strides on board a small ship, and the story moves on to the level of dream, or nightmare. He comes on a sailor, lying asleep on a bunk ('Mine! Mine!'), above him a picture — 'his woman's picture — smiling and smiling at the big sleeping man'. Thus the story finishes in a state of suspension as Ole Underwood is about to re-enact his tragedy of thirty years ago.

The fact that Ole Underwood is a sailor is relevant to the 'New Zealand' theme of the story. Like 'The Woman' and 'Millie', he is one of the dispossessed, but unlike them he is a wanderer, not tied to a restricting environment. His rootlessness is stressed even in the way he is described physically — his movements, for example, are always abrupt and restless. Katherine Mansfield is at some pains to emphasise that "E was a sailor till 'e married 'er', for Ole Underwood is a type of the immigrant adventurer, who hasn't succeeded in identifying himself with any particular community. No simple equation is made between his mental instability and his more fundamental insecurity, but, as in 'The Woman at the Store', the suggestion is there. In both stories the unnatural action of the central character is the result in part of an unnatural or unpropitious environment.

'Ole Underwood' is in this sense a New Zealand case-study, like 'Millie', 'The Woman at the Store', 'Old Tar'. This aspect of these stories has not been given enough attention. In the case of Ole Underwood, there is little doubt that Katherine Mansfield would have had in her mind as she wrote not merely the legendary figure of her childhood, but also a picture of her own grandfather, whom she later described in these terms in a letter to her young brother-in-law:

My grandpa said a man could travel all over the world with a clean pair of socks and a rook rifle. At the age of 70 odd he started for England thus equipped but Mother took fright and added a handkerchief or two. When he returned he was shorn of everything but a large watering can which he'd bought in London for his young marrows.[22]

She was aware of the fine line that separated her own ancestors, who had kept on the right side socially and financially, and figures like Ole Underwood, who had failed. The New Zealand stories written for *Rhythm* acknowledge a debt and recognise one kind of escape which had been made for her even before she was born.

The other stories which she contributed to *Rhythm* seem to have been mainly early work, 'pulled from a drawer' in Anthony Alpers's phrase when contributions were running short. Many of her early poems, and some of her earlier 'child' stories now emerged — 'The Little Girl', for example. Though these stories were in a sense the forerunners of the *Prelude*/'At the Bay' cycle, they are undistinguished in subject matter and treatment. For *The Blue Review* in 1913, she reverted to her satirical 'Elizabeth' style in the spa sketches 'Pension Seguin', 'Violet', 'Bains Turcs'. Though sophisticated in technique, these pieces remain essentially sterile. She seemed to have exhausted this particular vein for the present.

The time immediately after the collapse of *The Blue Review* was unproductive. It was not until 1915 that two unrelated events happened to crystallise her artistic aims. Up to this time her work had been uneven in quality and uncertain of direction; now she began to move more surely towards artistic self-definition. This was partly because of the arrival in England of her brother Leslie, in early 1915, to train for military service in the Great War. His appearance reminded her forcibly of the New Zealand home and family from which she had made such efforts to escape, and helped to clarify some of the reasons for her dissatisfaction with Murry and with the life she was leading in England. She began to write more sketches about her life in New Zealand, sensing perhaps that her strength as a writer must depend on trying to find some kind of accommodation between her past and her present, New Zealand and England, selves. Her work so far lacked unity and consistency because she had not yet found any unity of 'personality' or vision. She was, she later acknowledged, 'a divided being'. The first fruit of her attempt to overcome this division and discontinuity was *The Aloe*, drafted March–May 1915, in Paris.

1915 was also the year of *The Signature*. This was a short-lived 'little magazine' (in fact there were only three issues) written entirely by Katherine Mansfield, D. H. Lawrence, and Murry. Lawrence and Murry were both, at the time, intensely committed to the magazine, which was to express their private ideals and at the same time, and in so doing, to be a kind of public 'action' in the face of the war. Katherine Mansfield dissociated herself sharply from the venture, describing the stories which she contributed as simply 'the jam on the pill'. *The Signature* came to stand for something in both Lawrence and Murry to which she was utterly opposed. Even years later she wrote to Murry about something of his of which she disapproved, 'It's a *Signature* style of writing.' What she distrusted was the confessional, egoistical element in the work of both men. Murry's contribution to *The Signature* was entitled 'There Was a Little Man', a rambling, self-exploratory piece which may have enlightened him but is unlikely to have done as much for his readers. Lawrence's contribution was 'The Crown', now reprinted in *Phoenix II*. In 'The Crown' Katherine Mansfield found distilled the qualities of Lawrence's work to which she was most antipathetic, especially his looseness of style (she later commented cuttingly on the style of *The Lost Girl*: 'There is not one memorable *word*') and his didacticism. Though 'The Crown' is admittedly an essay, it is very closely tied to *The Rainbow*, and writing of the same nature occurs in many places both in this and other Lawrence novels.

From this style and approach Katherine Mansfield held herself aloof. She knew that she must write from her own experience, but felt that this could be achieved without intrusion of the authorial ego. She aimed to be 'least personal' when 'most herself':[23] this is the stance, the poise that informs all her best work. Her concern for style also intensified after the *Signature* period. The literary opposition between herself and Lawrence was thus fruitful for her, despite the personal difficulties of the alliance between the Lawrences and the Murrys. The proximity helped to clarify her own aims.

'The Wind Blows', printed in *The Signature* of 18 October 1915, is one of the very few of the early pieces to be included in the *Bliss* volume of 1920, and it was included because, she wrote, so many people, including Bertrand Russell and Virginia Woolf, had 'spoken strongly about it'. It describes a windy day in her home town of Wellington. The heroine, a young girl about the age of Laura in 'The Garden Party', is named Matilda ('Matilda Berry' was Katherine Mansfield's *nom de plume* in *The Signature*) and her brother, who, like Laura, she is extremely fond of, is called explicitly 'Bogey', the pet name for Leslie Beauchamp.

'The Wind Blows' is the most purely symbolist of her stories to this date. Many critics have commented on its power. An attentive reading shows that its strength lies in the care with which each detail of the story has been selected to have a symbolic as well as a narrative context.

The theme, which is never stated directly, but suggested through the images, is analogous to that of 'The Garden Party', though without that story's triumphant conclusion. Each of the three major symbols of the story is concerned with some aspect of Matilda's awakening into adulthood. The first, that of music, is associated with romantic love. In the only real event of the day, Matilda's music lesson, her youth and naïveté are stressed initially as she castigates 'the-girl-before-her' for blushing in front of the music teacher. Later, however, she too begins to melt under the influence of 'Mr Bullen's' sentimental kindness, and begins to cry, finding relief here from the tensions of home life:

> Mr Bullen takes her hands. His shoulder is there — just by her head. She leans on it ever so little, her cheek against the springy tweed.

The theme of initiation into adulthood is touched on, lightly. Mr Bullen 'says something about "waiting" and "marking time" and "that rare thing, a woman" ' — but there are also indications that this will not be the most crucial element either in the story or in Matilda's awakening. Mr Bullen's room is described as a 'cave'. It is a safe retreat from the storm outside, but there is also a barren, deadening air about both it and the kind of feeling which Mr Bullen has to offer. The point is made through the choice of details describing his room:

> It smells of art serge and stale smoke and chrysanthemums . . . there is a big vase of them on the mantelpiece behind the pale photograph of Rubenstein . . . *à mon ami*, Robert Bullen . . . Over the black glittering piano hangs 'Solitude' — a dark tragic woman draped in white, sitting on a rock, her knees crossed, her chin on her hands.

Outside, encircling the minor disturbance of the music lesson, are the wind and the risen sea. The sea as always in Mansfield denotes the mystery of life itself, inexhaustible, endless, impenetrable. On this particular day Bogey (who is near Matilda in age, for his voice is breaking) and Matilda both wish to go as near to the sea as possible — 'Come on! Come on! Let's get near!' They are eager for life, for its fullness and even its voracity:

> The sea is so high that the waves do not break at all; they thump against the rough stone wall and suck up the weedy, dripping steps.

It is this eagerness for life that draws them to the steamer which will help them to escape from their 'little town', and which will provide their passage into adulthood. It is an escape which, however, is deliberately left ambiguous:

> The wind does not stop her; she cuts through the waves, making for the open gate between the pointed rocks that leads to . . . [*ellipsis K.M.'s*]

From this point on, complexities and shadows multiply. Physically, it is suddenly dark — 'Now the dark stretches a wing over the tumbling water' — and the hopeful movement forward into life of Matilda and Bogey has somehow been arrested. The symbol which returns to close the story and finally envelop it is that of the wind, not an image of cheer. At the opening of the story, it is the wind that makes the day hideous, twisting and flattening the flowers in the next-door garden, shaking the iron on the roof of the house and rattling its windows. The bourgeois home environment and protective shell which seems inviolable to the child cannot be proof against this wind — as the mother comically wails, 'Now my best little Teneriffe-work teacloth is simply in ribbons!' The wind is elemental and outside human control. In the very early story-fantasies it images death (as in the last section of the early unfinished novel, *Juliet*), and its appearance in 'The Wind Blows' is an intimation if not of mortality at least of the dangers and perils of approaching adult life. The opening sentences of the story forecast this aspect of Matilda's initiation: the wind is 'nothing' only in the sense that it simply is, and images, the randomness of fate:

> Suddenly — dreadfully — she wakes up. What has happened? Something dreadful has happened. No — nothing has happened. It is only the wind shaking the house, rattling the windows, banging a piece of iron on the roof and making her bed tremble.

As in 'Ole Underwood' and 'The Woman at the Store', Katherine Mansfield employs colour in 'The Wind Blows' for expressive purposes. Rather, in this case, it is lack of colour, for the two dominant shades are black and white, and this is one of the reasons for the strange dream-like quality of the story. Neither colour is reassuring: the darkness, which intensifies at the end of the story, seems to close something off for ever; and white, which points to the future, is associated with a frightening solitude. One of the most insistent themes of the story is that of solitude, and the problem of 'living with oneself'. When Matilda wakes up at the opening of the story she is afraid to look at herself in the glass, and later she is frightened of being alone in her room, where the mirror gleams at her intimidatingly 'like the sky outside'. Only when her brother joins her, reinforcing her sense of identity, can she confront herself in the mirror:

Bogey's ulster is just like hers. Hooking the collar she looks at herself in the glass. Her face is white, they have the same excited eyes and hot lips. Ah, they know those two in the glass. Good-bye, dears; we shall be back soon.

Katherine Mansfield thus makes the point within the story that her brother's presence was necessary for its composition, giving her the security she needed for a confrontation with her past self and past experience. The sense of disturbance running through the story also testifies to the reality of the crisis surrounding her departure from New Zealand. Many critics have underplayed this, finding the diary entries relating to her departure mannered and overwrought, but there is no question that the break with home and family left a sense of insecurity which ran deep.

The passage quoted above, where brother and sister confront their mirror selves, and bid them farewell, anticipates the conclusion of the story:

A big black steamer with a long loop of smoke streaming, with the portholes lighted, with lights everywhere, is putting out to sea. The wind does not stop her; she cuts through the waves, making for the open gate between the pointed rocks that leads to . . . It's the light that makes her look so awfully beautiful and mysterious . . . *They* are on board leaning over the rail arm in arm.

'. . . Who are they?'

'. . . Brother and sister.'

'Look, Bogey, there's the town. Doesn't it look small? There's the post-office clock chiming for the last time. There's the esplanade where we walked that windy day. Do you remember? I cried at my music lesson that day — how many years ago! Good-bye, little island, good-bye . . .'

Now the dark stretches a wing over the tumbling water. They can't see those two any more. Good-bye, good-bye. Don't forget . . . But the ship is gone, now.

The wind — the wind.

As this passage opens, we are still on the time-level of the rest of the story, involved in an account of a specific day, with its ordinary and trivial events. However as, watching the steamer, brother and sister imagine their future selves, we are transported into their adult future when the same day is recalled affectionately from a long distance in time. As the 'children' become adults, they are simultaneously addressed by their childhood selves: 'Don't forget . . .' and as readers we become aware that it is this injunction, not to forget, which is being fulfilled in the very writing of the story. Something of the past has been recaptured by a narrator, like the narrator of Proust's *A la Récherche du Temps Perdu*, of whom we are now consciously aware; in consequence we are now aware also of the story as a literary construction. Our attention has been diverted, that is, away from the events as such and towards the complex process of their transmission.

'The Wind Blows' is thus a highly sophisticated and modernist story, blending certain elements of the earlier work, but achieving a new intensity. This is partly due to the New Zealand subject matter, but also to the ever more assured technique. Not only does Katherine Mansfield here employ the symbolist and Expressionist devices of earlier stories, but she uses present-tense narrative as a more active element in the story's meaning and structure. The sustained present tense of the narration is played off against its shifting time levels, involving us in the sense of loss and regret that pervades the close of the story.

'The Wind Blows' was written some months after the first drafting of *The Aloe*. During 1916 and 1917 *The Aloe* was extensively revised to form in *Prelude* the story which finally established Katherine Mansfield as a writer. *Prelude* was published in 1918 by Leonard and Virginia Woolf's Hogarth Press, and earned Virginia Woolf's somewhat reluctant praise. She defended it to her brother-in-law, Clive Bell:

> I only maintain that K.M.'s story has a certain quality as a work of art besides the obvious cleverness, which made it worth printing, and a good deal better than most stories anyway.[24]

Woolf's 'obvious cleverness' refers to the method of *Prelude*; its 'certain quality as a work of art' can perhaps be identified with the New Zealand subject matter. Writing of her past and her origins from the vantage point of the present, she was able in some measure to unite her 'divided selves' and give greater depth and resonance to her work.

The method of *Prelude* was innovatory for 1918 — four years before *Ulysses* and *Jacob's Room* were published. It is a symbolist method which was adopted quite consciously, as can be seen from the nature of the changes that were made as the 1915 version evolved into that of 1917. In returning to the symbolist ideals formulated in her early years, and in adapting them to short prose fiction, Katherine Mansfield effected a revolution in the short story comparable to that achieved by Joyce in the novel. Like novelists writing of Joyce, numerous short story writers have testified to her influence on the formal direction of the story.

Prelude can be described as symbolist firstly because in it, in accordance with Symbolist theory, the author conveys abstract states of mind or feeling only through concrete images, which act as 'objective correlatives'[25] for them. She rejects 'descriptive analysis' in favour of 'revelation through the slightest gesture', according to a prescription noted in one of her 1908 notebooks. In her work, this idea of the 'concrete image' through which emotion is to be expressed can be extended to include the composition of an entire story. Thus in her best writing each detail of character, setting and scene contributes to the evocation of a specific mood or feeling, and detail is not primarily mimetic.

She worked deliberately towards this art of exclusion and suggestion, as we can see by comparing the extant draft of *The Aloe* with *Prelude*.[26] The revisions that she made are almost always designed to eliminate analysis or explanation, so that themes are conveyed through the concrete texture of the story — through dramatic action, stylised interior monologue, scene and imagery. She repeatedly cut from *The Aloe* analysis of motive, so that her characters could be revealed, not explained. For example, this analysis of Linda Burnell's character as a child was excised:

People barely touched her; she was regarded as a cold, heart-
less little creature, but she seemed to have an unlimited
passion for that violent sweet thing called life — just being
alive and able to run and climb and swim in the sea and lie
in the grass.[27]

In *Prelude* the same information, and the reasons for the
deflection of Linda's vitality to within, are conveyed by
implication in the description of her early morning dream.

Prelude is also symbolist in its structure. Critics have normally
described the organisation of the story as 'random', seeing this as
her innovatory contribution to the art of the short story. In
reality, the story is anything but random. Each episode is played
off against the next to form a complex pattern of thematic
parallels and contrasts. In Sections V to VII, for example, the role
of woman is explored through a series of discriminations about
the affinities and differences between Linda Burnell (the central
figure), her mother Mrs Fairfield, and her sister Beryl. Linda's
status as a woman midway between her insecure, unmarried
sister and her stable and creative mother is affirmed through a
complex web of relationships. In Section VII, for example, Linda
is drawn momentarily to the moon, the symbol of chastity
normally associated with Beryl, which later accompanies Linda's
dream of escape from her married state as she contemplates the
aloe. But here Linda quickly shivers, and returns to sit by
Stanley's side, thus moving more towards acceptance of her
married state and becoming more like her mother. The section is
immediately followed by a scene with Beryl, alone only with her
'second self', having no Stanley to allay her fears and reassure her
about her own identity.

This use of parallelism and contrast is inseparable from the
patterns of imagery which prevade the story, extending to
almost every detail, down to the up-ended tables and chairs of the
opening paragraphs. The main image of the story, as the title of
the first draft suggests, is the aloe. That its exact 'meaning' has
never been agreed on is evidence of its continuing power to stir
and disturb the imagination of the reader. Recent critics have
suggested, diversely, that the aloe is either a 'phallic tree of

knowledge', or an image of female sexuality, especially attractive to Linda because of its infrequency of bearing. Just because the aloe can admit of either interpretation — and of many others — a more inclusive and flexible reading seems necessary. In the full context of the story the aloe emerges most convincingly as an image of the fundamental life-force itself, including sexual force in human life. It represents the essential will or energy behind appearance, which is why not all the characters of the story approach it, for not all are capable of penetrating to the deeper issues of life. Stanley Burnell, for instance, and the precocious and bossy sister Isobel are excluded. In those who do approach the aloe, it arouses conflicting feelings. The young Kezia is struck especially by its aged and unlovely aspect. Linda is led by its appearance to focus instantly on the central issue in her life, the dread of having children. Yet both Linda and Kezia see something hidden in the aloe, the possibility of its flowering. The potential flowering of the aloe foreshadows the 'flowering of the self' which will occur for Linda in 'At the Bay' (the sequel conceived at the same time as *Prelude*), in the moment when she forgets herself and discovers love for her son.

Katherine Mansfield described such a flowering of the self in a journal entry of 1920:

> . . . a self which is continuous and permanent; which . . . thrusts a scaled bud through years of darkness until, one day, the light discovers it and shakes the flower free and — we are alive — we are flowering for our moment upon the earth. This is the moment which, after all, we live for — the moment of direct feeling when we are most ourselves and least personal.

Through the controlling symbol of the aloe Katherine Mansfield thus expresses in *Prelude* a view of life which underlies all her major stories. The aloe is, like life itself, often unlovely and cruel, offering for long periods nothing but 'years of darkness', yet it also holds within itself the possibility of that rare flowering which justifies existence, 'which, after all, we live for'.

The other images of the story blend into and support this central symbol. That of flowering, for example, occurs in other contexts than that of the aloe. It appears in Beryl's moonlit dream of love when she is offered a fantastic bouquet of 'bright waxy flowers', symbolising the falsity of her romantic expectations. Several images are counter-pointed: the flower and the weed, sunlight and moonlight, material goods and spiritual light (the 'little lamp' of the grandmother, an image which reappears, of course, in 'The Doll's House'). The image of the bird or duck is set against that of the aloe, and acquires particularly complex overtones. On one level, it suggests escape and freedom, as when Beryl runs off gaily in the early morning, singing:

> How many thousand birds I see
> That sing aloud from every tree . . .

but soon Beryl stops singing to add savagely, 'One may as well rot here as anywhere else.' Similarly in Linda's early morning dream, a bird shown to her by her father at first seems sweet and charming, and, we are told, 'It was quite tame.' Yet 'a funny thing happened'; the bird swells and grows and objectifies Linda's fears, becoming a baby 'with a gaping bird-mouth, opening and shutting'. For Beryl, the bird symbolises an escape which can only be illusory in her present circumstances. For Linda, the bird grows rapidly out of control, as does Stanley, who has been her 'escape' in Beryl's terms. Through the image of the duck, the suggestions of both bird images are expressed more unambiguously. The duck is a bird, and as such is something winged and potentially free. However, it is doomed to be destroyed by Stanley's force, or by that of his surrogate, Pat (Pat's executioner's role is foreshadowed at the beginning of the story: his clothes hang from the door-peg 'like a hanged man'; and at his side, on the floor, is 'an empty cane bird-cage'). Stanley's will also controls the lives of the two sisters, and the duck scene (Section IX) thus represents, in the worst possible light, what he is doing to Linda and Beryl — he is 'destroying' them by forcing Linda into unwanted childbearing, and by moving Beryl away from the town where she might find her longed-for suitor. Yet Stanley's strength is also opposed by something in Linda, and the decapitation of the duck is also an objectified expression of a repressed desire of hers, for it suggests castration — earlier in the story, in the morning scene between Stanley and Linda, we are told that Stanley looks to Linda just like 'a big fat turkey'.

The decapitation of the duck thus balances the scenes involving the aloe. The aloe, though fearful in appearance, is a positive force, with potential for flowering and fruitfulness. The scene with the duck focusses on the destructive and aggressive impulses of the adult characters, and is wholly negative in its implications.

Prelude is elegant, concentrated, and unified. Its 'images' merge seamlessly with the narrative structure, in the manner which was to become characteristic of Katherine Mansfield's story art. The avoidance of rhetoric and polemic is also characteristic. When she first wrote *The Aloe* in Paris she included many passages of feminist polemic, partly no doubt because she was seeing a great deal of Beatrice Hastings at the time. When she came to revise it, all such writing was carefully pruned away — for example, a complete scene describing Mrs Trout's tea-time visit to her sisters Linda and Beryl was cut, because it included a good deal of special pleading on behalf of women.

From this time on she avoided polemical writing, adhering to the Symbolist belief in art as an autotelic activity. In this and other ways suggested above *Prelude* represents a complete return to — or the first complete embodiment of — the symbolist aesthetic developed so early on in her notebooks. Her years of experiment ended with *Prelude*: in the course of the two years spent working on it she fully 'realised' her method.

In 1917, she published a handful of sketches which do not quite fit in with this account of her development: 'Two Tuppenny Ones, Please', 'Late at Night' and 'The Black Cap'. These were part of a series of what she called her 'light' pieces for *The New Age*. The most striking thing about them is that all three are in near-monologue form. 'Two Tuppenny Ones' is a monologue with a silent interlocutor; 'Late at Night' is pure monologue; 'The Black Cap' is mainly monologue except for a few brief exchanges with the stolid husband. In these pieces, she is not experimenting with dramatisation of character or with the imitation of natural speech rhythms. She had already shown in *Prelude* that she could dramatise character far more effectively by more indirect means. She is exploring something more interesting, the problem of the author's 'voice', and is attempting, though in crude form as yet, to let the 'hidden' author emerge more openly into the text, approaching the audience more nearly. It is a problem that she abandoned for a time after these attempts ('Je ne parle pas français' is a rather different kind of work: its first-person narrator is stylishly characterised and kept at a distance), but she took it up again in 1921–22 stories like 'A Married Man's Story', 'A Bad Idea' and 'The Canary'. In these stories she created an effect of more naked 'utterance' than in any other of her works: this effect will be discussed in more detail later.

3 The South of France 1918-20

In late 1917 Katherine Mansfield was advised to leave England for a warmer climate. This she promptly did, despite the difficulties of travelling through wartime France, and arrived in early 1918 in Bandol, the scene of her first 'idyll' with Murry. The painful separation from Murry (who couldn't get permission to leave England in wartime) was repeated in the winters of 1919–20 and 1920–21, this time because of his editorial commitment to *The Athenaeum*.

The 1918 stay in Bandol was a cruel parody of her 1916 visit. The conditions of war had changed the town out of recognition and even the journey to the place was a nightmare. She described it in a letter:

> The soldiers demanded the train — and that *les civils* should evacuate it. Not with good temper, but furious — very ugly — and VILE. They banged on the windows, wrenched open the doors and threw out the people and their luggage after them. They came to our carriage, swarmed in — told the officers they too must go, and one of them caught hold of me as though I were a sort of packet of rugs. I never said a word for I was far too tired and vague to care about anything . . .[1]

Yet under harsh conditions, only a month after she had arrived she had completed the long story 'Je ne parle pas français' and two weeks later 'Bliss'. And this after a long period of comparative silence during which she had written nothing apart from her revisions of *The Aloe* and a few sketches for *The New Age*. Both 'Je ne parle pas français' and 'Bliss' represent a breakthrough, in different ways, and the achievement is the more striking in that they were written in a position of complete isolation and under the stress of actual physical hardship. This was a pattern which was to be repeated, or rather it was one which had already been established, with the writing of *The Aloe* while she was living alone in Paris under air-raid attacks in 1915. Throughout the period up to 1920 her best work seems to have come from periods when she was isolated both socially and intellectually. Thus 'The Man without a Temperament' was composed during a period of extreme solitude and alienation at Ospedaletti in 1919 and the following winter she produced some of her most successful stories in Menton before Murry's arrival. Only a few stories of any quality came from England: these would include 'This Flower' and 'The Escape', written at Hampstead in the summers of 1919 and 1920 respectively.

She seems to have courted isolation for her work, even to have welcomed certain restrictions. At two key points, in 1915 and again in 1919, she expressed her sense that she worked best under external constraints, using the image of a caged bird:

> As always happens I am now so tied and bound, so *caged*, that I know I'll *sing*. I'm just on the point of writing something awfully good, if you know that feeling.[2]

> Oh it is agony to meet corruption when one thinks all is fair — the big snail under the leaf — the spot in the child's lung — what a *wicked, wicked* God! But it is more than useless to cry out. Hanging in our little cages on the awful wall over the gulf of eternity we must sing — sing.[3]

Mansfield makes no conceptual distinction here between the artist and the ordinary man. Her cage is not the palace of art and she does not refer here to the formal constraints which make for 'artificial' shape and beauty in song. The cage is the cage of circumstance and contingency, common to all men who have intelligence enough to see the boundaries and limitations of existence. It is this awareness which makes man able, and which impels the artist, to 'sing'. And as the net of circumstance tightens, so the artistic impulse is strengthened. Katherine Mansfield thus follows romantic tradition in relating artistic creativity to suffering and lack. Keats made the same connection in his letters using similar imagery of the clipped wings of the bird and of the prison. She was also following Nietzsche, one of her early mentors, in stressing the relationship between creativity and suffering. It was he who wrote in a famous passage:

> I have often asked myself, whether I am not much more deeply indebted to the hardest years of my life than to any others . . . And as to my prolonged illness — do I not owe much more to it than I do to my health? To it I owe a higher kind of health . . . *To it I owe even my philosophy* . . . great suffering is the ultimate emancipator of spirit.[4]

Katherine Mansfield testified to the insight which came from suffering in several letters to Murry, and presented 'tragic knowledge' (a phrase from a 1919 letter) as the key to her art in the period 1918–20.

The emphasis changed and the perspective broadened in the final two years. A comparison of the following passages from letters may briefly illustrate this shift in emphasis:

> And then suffering, bodily suffering such as I've known for three years. It has changed for ever everything — even the *appearance* of the world is not the same — there is something added. *Everything has its shadow.* Is it right to resist such suffering? Do you know I feel it has been an immense privilege.[5]

> Laura says, 'But all these things must not happen at once.' And Life answers, 'Why not? How are they divided from each other.' And they *do* all happen, it is inevitable. And it seems to me there is beauty in that inevitability.[6]

'Bliss' was completed on 28 February 1918, and was the first story in which the symbolist method of *Prelude* was employed in condensed form, in a story with a single main action and character. 'Bliss' also established Katherine Mansfield as one of the moderns. It was widely read when it first appeared in *The English Review* and was later taken up by T. S. Eliot as an example of the modern temper in a discussion in *After Strange Gods*.[7] We can now see that its dense, imagistic structure links it closely with the contemporary poetry of Eliot and Pound, and interestingly 'Prufrock' (1917) was described by Mansfield as 'after all a short story',[8] suggesting an awareness on her part of affinities of method and content.

'Bliss' has been much commented on, and its sexual theme in particular much debated by critics. There are two kinds of reservation about the story. Some readers have found it 'disagreeable' or 'cruel',[9] while others have found it shallow, most notably Virginia Woolf who described the story as 'not the vision of an interesting mind'.[10] This latter comment is revealing both of Woolf's attitude to fiction in general and of a faulty reading of 'Bliss'. The appeal of 'Bliss' is precisely not to or from 'the mind'. The author aimed to write a symbolist story in which meaning could not be apprehended or summarised discursively. Thus meaning is disclosed in 'Bliss' entirely through the disposition of language and image in a highly organised, tangibly affective text. The analogy with the operation of a lyric is pertinent. It is a point which has been made before, but its implications have not always been followed up rigorously.

The charge of cruelty or disagreeableness stems from a related point, the lack of a clearly defined authorial presence in the story. Katherine Mansfield effaces the narrator-figure as nearly as possible, leaving the text and its network of images to 'speak for itself'. The absence of a controlling 'metalanguage' to direct our responses may consequently create a sense of moral or ethical vacuum. Again, close reading is necessary for appreciation of the technique of muted direction which gives the story its very definite moral edge.

'Bliss' revolves around the character of Bertha Young, a fashionable married woman of thirty. The story turns on the theme of maturity, as Bertha's name might suggest. It is a double pun, pointing both to her immaturity — she is indeed young for her years — but also to possibilities of rebirth and potential moral and spiritual development.

The story is cast in indirect free form, the narrator's voice merging with the thoughts, the vocabulary, the very mode of perception of the central character. The method is exemplified in the opening sentence:

Although Bertha Young was thirty she still had moments like this when she wanted to run instead of walk, to take dancing steps on and off the pavement, to bowl a hoop, to throw something up in the air and catch it again, or to stand still and laugh at — nothing — at nothing, simply.

We see Bertha in the act of making sense of her experiences, verbalising them and then testing her own descriptions against the imaginary audience for whom she is always performing, usually with a sense of inadequacy. The author explained this process in a letter to Murry of 14 March 1918:

> What I *meant* (I hope it don't sound high falutin') was Bertha, not being an artist, was yet artist manquée enough to realise that these words and expressions were not and couldn't be hers. They were, as it were, *quoted* by her, borrowed with . . . an eyebrow . . . yet she'd none of her own.[11]

Such words and phrases — 'at nothing, simply', 'the most amusing orange coat', 'so incredibly beautiful' — occur at intervals throughout the text, creating the intended effect of discrepancy when juxtaposed with Bertha's more immediate and more naturally phrased perceptions: ' "What creepy things cats are!" she stammered.'

The first sentence of the story suggests Bertha's immaturity (*although* she is thirty, she still wishes to behave like a child) but does not confirm it, and this is a structural movement which is repeated throughout the text. One of the first things we notice about Bertha's discourse is that she 'knows', on a subconscious level, far more than she will concede. Her patterns of thought and her 'borrowed language' are means of evading knowledge and of preserving her innocence at all costs:

> Really — really — she had everything. She was young. Harry and she were as much in love as ever, and they got on together splendidly and were really good pals. She had an adorable baby. They didn't have to worry about money. They had this absolutely satisfactory house and garden. And friends —

> modern, thrilling friends, writers and painters and poets or
> people keen on social questions — just the kind of friends
> they wanted . . .
>
> Harry had such a zest for life. Oh, how she appreciated it
> in him. And his passion for fighting — for seeking in every-
> thing that came up against him another test of his power and
> of his courage — that, too, she understood. Even when it
> made him just occasionally, to other people, who didn't know
> him well, a little ridiculous perhaps . . . For there were
> moments when he rushed into battle where no battle was . . .

The game is given away by those dashes and ellipses which
indicate the hesitations before Bertha finds the healing phrase to
gloss over the relationships she is considering. Her discourse thus
simultaneously conceals and reveals the truth. Realities are
suggested in other ways. Bertha's virginal frigidity, for example,
is revealed not only in her own terms — 'She'd been in love with
him, of course, in every other way, but just not in that way' —
but also by the somewhat inappropriate application of the word
'bridegroom' to her husband of several years, and by the ironic
identification of herself and her baby ('Little B').

The question of maturity takes on a deeper resonance when
we consider the other members of the cast of Bertha's little
dinner party, or 'play by Tchekhof'. Two of the dinner guests,
the Norman Knights, mirror the relationship obtaining between
Bertha and Harry. Their nicknames are the interchangeable 'Face'
and 'Mug', and they are such good pals that they are by now
indistinguishable from each other — that is, sexless. Eddie
Warren is the pale and decorative youth who should most
fittingly pair off with Pearl Fulton (the same silver/white imagery
is associated with both). But Pearl Fulton is the joker in the pack.
She says almost nothing, and does not even look at the other
guests — it is as though 'she lived by listening rather than seeing'.
She is thus the only character in the story who does not define
her very presence in it by a characteristic form of speech and the
use of sprightly contemporary jargon, and this seems to suggest a
maturity which the others lack. However, the effect that she has
on Harry, as perceived by Bertha in the moment when she

discovers the relationship between her husband and her friend, is not exactly elevating:

> His lips said 'I adore you', and Miss Fulton laid her moonbeam fingers on his cheeks and smiled her sleepy smile. Harry's nostrils quivered: his lips curled back in a hideous grin while he whispered: 'To-morrow', and with her eyelids Miss Fulton said: 'Yes'.

Bertha's immaturity is primarily sexual, but it seems that sexual maturity and knowledge do not necessarily bring maturity in other ways. Harry and Pearl Fulton are shown as unremarkable, even shoddy, human beings, and their purely sensual relationship is felt to be as incomplete as the sexless companionship of 'Face' and 'Mug'. The exact irony of the story is that of all the characters it is Bertha who has the most capacity for growth and maturity. Her suppressed but real sexual force is indicated in the fire and sun imagery which dominates the first half of the story, until the turning point where the drawing-room fire dies down to a 'nest of *baby phoenixes*' (our italics). After this, Pearl Fulton and her moon imagery are in the ascendant, and Bertha's rebirth becomes problematic.

Bertha also has a certain degree of intellectual and artistic potential. She is capable of discriminations beyond the range of her circle of friends, as we see in her response to the still life she creates in her drawing room (the still life which is within her control as the drama enacted later is not):

> Mary brought in the fruit on a tray and with it a glass bowl, and a blue dish, very lovely, with a strange sheen on it as though it had been dipped in milk . . .
> When she had finished with them and had made two pyramids of these bright round shapes, she stood away from the table to get the effect — and it really was most curious. For the dark table seemed to melt into the dusky light and the glass dish and the blue bowl to float in the air . . .

Her development is blocked by the circumstances of a life which she herself has created. It was the young and immature Bertha who chose the husband who now constrains and defines her. His coarseness not only checks the birth of her desire for him very obviously in the course of the story but also by implication throughout their married life. It also determines the intellectual level on which she lives, among a circle of friends not sufficiently intelligent to enable her to develop such abilities as she does possess. She is, as Mansfield pointed out, that most pitiable of creatures, the 'artist manquée' of the type analysed by Thomas Mann, condemned to suffer from sensibilities and perceptions which she lacks the drive and talent to use constructively.

In theory, however, after Bertha's 'revelation' almost any line of development is open to her. One question which has been raised is that of her 'latent homosexuality'. Many critics have felt this to be a genuine element in the story, pointing out that it is the touch of Pearl Fulton which 'fans, starts blazing' Bertha's fire of bliss. The following passage has also been noted:

> But now — ardently! ardently! The word ached in her ardent body! Was this what that feeling of bliss had been leading up to? But then, then —

Does Bertha's ellipsis here indicate a suppressed recognition that the 'fire of bliss' has more to do with Pearl Fulton than her husband? This is one possible reading, but it is also possible to see the ellipsis, and the whole process, as more complex. Bertha acts, after all, as Harry's procuress — it is she who 'finds' Pearl Fulton for him, and she has also had other 'women finds'. This could suggest voyeuristic rather than lesbian characteristics, and this makes more credible the sudden birth of desire in Bertha, as it takes place when she is for the first time in the presence of Pearl Fulton and her husband for an extended period of time.

Bertha's relationship with Pearl reflects, it may be, one future possibility; that with her husband certainly another. Somewhere between these three central characters the story seems to propose some new arrangement — a 'solution' and development. We can legitimately speculate, for the story is without closure:

'Your lovely pear tree — pear tree — pear tree!'

Bertha simply ran over to the long windows.

'Oh, what is going to happen now?' she cried.

But the pear tree was as lovely as ever and as full of flower and as still.

Yet through its internal structure — through repetition of imagery, juxtaposition and parallelism, the word-play — the text itself leads us to the inevitable conclusion that the most likely change for Bertha will be that of no change. The last paragraph of the story shows us the technique of muted direction in miniature. In the passage quoted above it is, as so often in the story, through diction and articulation that meaning is released. It is the conscious naïveté of Bertha's final appeal which suggests that she will continue to evade responsibility and knowledge, retreating from revelation into denial and repression. Like the pear tree, Bertha is, at the age of thirty, 'becalmed' and rooted — but she is not, and seems fated never to be, 'in fullest, richest bloom'.

To what extent can 'Bliss' be called tragic? Murry would link it with 'Je ne parle pas français' as an expression of Katherine Mansfield's 'negative kick-off' in writing, a 'cry against corruption'. Despite the manifest absurdity of his division of her writing into two simple categories, there is a close link between these particular stories, written within weeks of each other. First, they are linked thematically in that both deal with a dual betrayal involving a husband or lover and a friend. The setting is also similar. Both explore the social milieu in which the aspiring artist and the bourgeois meet: compare for example the description of Raoul Duquette's meeting with Dick Harmon and the dinner party scene of 'Bliss'. The relationship between the artist and the bourgeois is seen as mutually corrupting in such circumstances, for the one seeks direct financial reward, the other a questionable social status, from the contact.

It is because Bertha Young is firmly placed as a socialising 'patron' that 'Bliss' is not tragic in the usual sense of the word, for our sympathies are necessarily alienated to a certain extent from such a person. Yet this social placement is the key to Katherine Mansfield's more personal kind of 'tragic vision'. For her, tragedy lay to a large degree in the inevitable. Her philosophy is fundamentally deterministic, and so it is that in 'Bliss' we see Bertha trapped by character and environment as surely as Raoul Duquette in 'Je ne parle pas français'. Even more so: she resists the self-knowledge which he does at least possess, and she cannot even write her story.

'Je ne parle pas français' is difficult to approach without some knowledge of its biographical circumstances. When Middleton Murry claimed that it contained a personal symbolism only he could understand, he was no doubt thinking about more of its features than the resemblance of Raoul Duquette to Francis Carco, the French writer with whom Katherine Mansfield had enjoyed an escapade three years before, in 1915. 'The fate of the Mouse, caught in the toils of the world's evil, abandoned by her lover,' wrote Murry, 'is Katherine's fate.'[12] But it is doubtful if even Murry himself saw it in quite such simply autobiographical terms as that. He compared his reaction to it with his feeling on reading the Russian author Fyodor Dostoevsky's *Letters from the Underworld* and must have seen not just the connection between Dostoevsky's underworld and what Duquette calls his 'submerged world', but also the link between Dostoevsky's writer (the title of whose book can more accurately be translated 'Notes from the mouse-hole') and Katherine Mansfield's 'Mouse'. Dostoevsky was very much in the minds of both Mansfield and Murry at this time. The autobiographical elements are far more thoroughly diffused through the story than is admitted in Murry's plain equation of Katherine with the Mouse.

We can identify a little of this diffusion by looking at Duquette's self-characterisation as the story's narrator. 'Je ne parle pas français' was almost the only major story Katherine Mansfield wrote as a narrative in the first person, and her narrator is certainly one of the most complex of all the dramatic roles she constructed. Raoul Duquette is in concentrated form all the aspects of the 'free artist' which she had witnessed, as much in herself as in anyone from Bohemian Paris. Through Duquette she explores some of the assumptions and forms of behaviour which had influenced the evolution of her own art.

He begins by describing human personalities — and therefore his own self, and his art, his story — as portmanteaux. People become their packaging, the roles they act.

> How can one look the part and not be the part? Or be the part and not look it? Isn't looking — being? Or being — looking? At any rate, who is to say it is not?

he demands, aware that he is posturing before his mirror and readers. The same assertion of art as self-development is apparent in his rejection of his own childhood, and of all nostalgic ties. Life is the freedom of the present moment.

> There I emerged, came out into the light, and put out my two horns with a study and a bedroom and a kitchen on my back.

So he writes about life in the 'submerged world' of his Paris and his version of Dostoevsky's mousehole.

There is a great deal of Katherine Mansfield's own postures as a free artist in this self-portrait by Duquette. Self-parody shapes the construction of the whole story to an extent very difficult to calculate precisely. Duquette is shaping his narrative as an epiphany, a revelation springing from a 'cued moment' or *'geste'* (sign). To him the point of his story is not the poor trapped Mouse that Murry saw but the moment of recognition that brings him to life as an artist. At the point of recognition,

> I opened my eyes very wide. There I had been for all eternity, as it were, and now at last I was coming to life . . .

And of course he is the work of art he creates, his own finished narrative, 'Je ne parle pas français'. Katherine Mansfield is playing games with her own theories of literary creation. The difficulty of locating where Duquette ends and she begins makes the story without question the most complex and inaccessible in her entire *oeuvre*.

It is built in twenty sections, which we might conveniently divide into five main steps, rather like the scene and act divisions of a play. The first act has four sections or scenes of which the first and longest leads up to the cued moment, Duquette's discovery of the title phrase scrawled on the café's writing pad. The second and third scenes affirm the writer's rejection of any past, and the fourth describes the beginning of his life as a free writer. This act contains the passages quoted above as evidence for Duquette as Katherine Mansfield's self-parody.

The second act is the account of Duquette's meeting with Dick and his development of the faithful fox-terrier role, up to the point of his arrival at the railway station to meet Dick when he returns to Paris with Mouse. The third act is the meeting at the station, followed by the hotel and tea, up to the point when Dick leaves Mouse alone with the benign-seeming puppy. The fourth act is his fox-terrier gambols around Mouse and the discovery that Dick has fled. Finally there are four short scenes, the fifth act, beginning with Mouse's escape from the dog, and returning to the narrator at his cued moment.

Each of the four parts of the final act involves a breach of the ethos Duquette proclaimed in the opening sections. In the first he is forced to admit that he cannot sustain acting the benign fox-terrier — 'of course I knew that I couldn't have kept it up'. It isn't always possible to be the part one plays. In the second, which begins 'But how she makes me break my rule', he fantasises a nostalgic childhood with her. Nostalgia is against his rules, but he needs it, just as he needs to return to the café which was the locality for his *geste*. In the third, the local realities of the café in which he enjoys the cued moment break in and drive him to the opposite pose, the sham whose relationship with Mouse is that of procurer for 'some dirty old gallant'. He is less free, less in control of his own play-acting, than his ethos requires. The very short final section reaffirms the cued moment characteristic of epiphanies, and equally pointedly reasserts the fox-terrier symbol.

> I must go. I must go. I reach down my coat and hat. Madame knows me. 'You haven't dined yet?' she smiles. 'No, not yet, Madame.'

The story thus ends with Duquette poised at the point of

departure from the scene of the cued moment. The pink writing-pad with its green scrawl, 'Je ne parle pas français', will be left behind. Its moment is now past and preserved in the artist's narrative. And the narrative is left, a carefully framed anecdote, framed in distortion because the narrator's Modernist pose has been displayed in its fractured misalignment, and the more revealing because the frame and therefore the perspective on the story has been so distinctly affirmed by the distortions.

The story swings from the self-portrait of Duquette the free Modernist, through the fox-terrier's games with his prey — first Dick and then Mouse — back to the Modernist and what is now to be seen clearly as his self-creating role-playing. The story has at its core not 'the fate of the Mouse', as Murry saw it, but the portrait of the Modernist artist, the actor whose principles also make him a gigolo and a pimp, who sees life as 'an old hag to be throttled' but who in fact is no Raskolnikov — he cannot literally commit murder like the hero of Dostoevsky's *Crime and Punishment*. He is the artist as predator, ruthlessly feeding his experiences into his art. He upholds the Modernist principle of rejecting analysis and so will not examine his own poses. Having first seen himself as Madame Butterfly waiting to hear news of the return of Dick, his Pinkerton, he readily puts Mouse into the Madame Butterfly role, with Dick the Pinkerton figure abandoning her to her fate. Everything is a pose, a portmanteau. His discovery that Dick and Mouse are truly suffering delights him because it gives the game a new level of realism. His *geste* is not merely realistic, but true. His experience, concentrated into the cued moment, becomes his art.

As with any dramatic monologue, it is not possible to separate the narrator from his narrative. The story he tells, of the disastrous collapse of Dick's and Mouse's escapade together, is primarily an account of himself. It is an account of failures. For all the central epiphany, it is a series of misunderstandings and blurred communications. Starting with the title phrase itself, Duquette's story is one of spasmodic, reluctant connections. He is a Parisian, inhabiting a carnivorous jungle,

as though we were some kind of many-headed monster, and

Paris behind us nothing but a great trap we had set to catch these sleepy innocents.

One side of his fox-terrier image of himself is the carnivorous monster. But even that act is muddled and inconsistent. The author of *False Coins, Wrong Doors, Left Umbrellas* is more inclined to fumble than to devour. He cannot even communicate perfectly with himself. At the end of the second section of the introductory act he presents himself as a faithful dog waiting for his lost Mouse to return.

All the while I wrote that last page my other self has been chasing up and down out in the dark there. It left me just when I began to analyse my grand moment, dashed off distracted, like a lost dog who thinks at last, at last, he hears the familiar step again.

In his narrative Duquette follows the lost-dog acknowledgement of his imperfectly packed portmanteau with accounts of his relations with women. The African laundress of his childhood, the women he serves as a gigolo, all supply relationships which he holds at the sexual level only, until he comes upon Dick Harmon. Dick is characterised by his song, which Duquette quotes but inevitably only half comprehends. And their friendship itself is described in primarily sexual terms: 'It was he who made the first advances.' Dick was the fish who came 'right out of the water after the bait'. When Dick returns to England Duquette is the woman, the Madame Butterfly abandoned by her lover. Before Dick reappears in the company of Mouse Duquette has brushes with his concierge and with the couple on the Métro (an anecdote which has the ring of authenticity, and might well have been one of Carco's own stories about himself). Then comes the game with Dick and Mouse, and the transfer of roles from fox-terrier puppy (female) with Dick to fox-terrier (predator) playing with Mouse.

She had been so tame, so confiding, letting me, at any rate spiritually speaking, hold her tiny quivering body in one hand and stroke her furry head.

But inevitably for such an imperfect communicator, he loses her. None of his communications in life is better than an abortive attempt at control of other beings. In the end he is left day-dreaming about a role he could not sustain, holding only the pointed phrase, the denial of affinity with anything Parisian, 'Je ne parle pas français'.

Paris is the city of art, and it is for this reason that its inhabitants are explicitly presented as carnivores, waiting for the approach of the 'innocents' on whose experience they may feed. The artist lives vicariously, always on the look-out for material. He is detached from his emotions almost before they have developed, as in Duquette's 'grand moment' in the café. This separation between the artist and his feelings is both necessary for his art and potentially destructive of it. On the other hand, the gap between Duquette and the people surrounding him is destructive in simple human terms. Unable to distinguish between a fiction and a reality, he is rendered incapable of necessary action, perpetually impotent, in the classic position of the artist as voyeur.

We should therefore be ready to condemn Duquette both as man and as artist, if it were not for his edgy awareness of the inadequacy of his feelings, and his recurrent excursions into sentiment and nostalgia. As he breaks the 'rules' which he has made for himself he increasingly engages the reader's sympathy, as if he were a self-deluding cripple. And it is the tension between the rules and his breaking of them which makes possible the precarious, unstable achievement of the narrative itself, 'Je ne parle pas français'.

Katherine Mansfield wrote 'The Man without a Temperament' in January 1920 at Ospedaletti, during the deepest crisis of depression that she suffered. It was her attempt to set down her absent husband's position, his role in relation to his sick wife, and its implications for his character. Her diary entry for 10 January 1920 reads

Thought out *The Exile* [i.e., 'The Man without a Temperament'].

Appalling night of misery, deciding that J. had no more need of our love.[13]

Since it presents the situation she was demanding Murry should adopt — a man exiled from his home and his roots by the need to stay in a warm climate with his invalid wife — and does so from the husband's perspective, it can be seen as in part her attempt at empathy, at reaching towards an objective truth through art.

Her position, she felt, was desperately deprived. A letter to Murry written from Ospedaletti six weeks earlier had described her own reaction to her illness:

> Once the defences are fallen between you and Death they are not built up again. It needs such a little push, hardly that, just a false step, just not looking, and you are over. Mother, of course, lived in this state for years. Ah, but she lived *surrounded*. She had her husband, her children, her home, her friends, physical presences, darling treasures to be cherished — and I've not one of these things. I have only my work.[14]

She used her work — 'The Man without a Temperament' — as a way of clarifying this situation and giving it a perspective which would not be twisted by her desperate depression. She had not long before sent Murry a letter which voiced her misery and her anger against him, in the poem 'The New Husband'. It begins

> Someone came to me and said
> Forget, forget that you've been wed.
> Who's your man to leave you be
> Ill and cold in a far country?
> Who's the husband — who's the stone
> Could leave a child like you alone?

This poem brought him out to Ospedaletti for two weeks over Christmas. 'The Man without a Temperament' was written a few days after he went back to London and to his job editing *The Athenaeum*. The question of whether he should give up his editorship and join her was still unresolved. Seen biographically, then, the story is her response to the unresolved question. But it is, of course, much more than that.

The original title for the story, 'The Exile', belongs more distinctly with the initial impulse to describe Murry's position than with the finished product. The husband is indeed exiled from London, and has the yearnings which go with exile. During the story his mind reverts three times to the land he has left, in explicit nostalgia. There are flashbacks to England in the snow, to the English country in November, the countryside with home and friends, and to the late summer day in London when the doctor gave his verdict for exile. The husband's alienation from everyone in the warm south, the guests at the *pension*, the servants, the local children and the old women washing their linen, contrasts with his sense of being at home among the literati of England.

> In the drawing-room; Jinnie is sitting pretty nearly in the fire. 'Oh, Robert, I didn't hear you come in. Did you have a good time? How nice you smell! A present?' 'Some bits of black-berry I picked for you. Pretty colour.' 'Oh, lovely, Robert! Dennis and Beaty are coming to supper.' Supper — cold beef, potatoes in their jackets, claret, household bread. They are gay — everybody's laughing. 'Oh, we all know Robert,' says Dennis, breathing on his eyeglasses and polishing them. 'By the way, Dennis, I picked up a very jolly little edition of . . .'

In the *pension*, nobody can know Robert. He is the complete alien. Nonetheless, the final title, like the story itself, suggests much more than the portrait of an exile.

The man without roots is a man without a self, capable of sustaining a pose, a secondary, serving and nursing role, but with no life and therefore no temperament of his own. In a letter to Murry written in March 1918 Katherine Mansfield had registered the need for roots. Juliette, her maid in Bandol, was strong because she had *des racines*. Roots are the basis for the strong honesty of a Wordsworth.[15] The rootless life of exiles like the man without a temperament is one bound by deception and evasions.

While the character-sketches of the guests at the *pension* underline the husband's exile, the images emphasise his loss of ego. The most conspicuous, repeated symbol has him revolving the heavy ring on his finger, registering the bond which keeps him in his rootless exile, while he does nothing but stand by the hall door like a servant waiting to be summoned for duty. He revolves the ring obsessively through the day, until at the close his wife turns it for him while she asks for his reassurance that he does not resent his exile with her. Not even his obsessive twitches are his own. The ring starts as a symbol of his captivity, and ends by evoking his denial of his ego. It brings out the contrast which is basic to the story between the choice he has made, of self-control and a suppressed ego, and the choice he has forsaken, of his own world and its opportunities for happy self-expression.

The other symbols underline the related contrasts. The wife's footsteps drag lightly, while he alternates between stasis and haste, and yet it is she who takes his watch when he goes for a walk and she, who has nothing in her life but to observe time passing, is the one who records that he is three minutes late coming back. He is all the life she has, and she measures his absences. At night she is the enormous white moon, pure as in conventional moon imagery, laid out in the moonlight in one of the two separate beds, her hands crossed like a white corpse. By contrast he is the silent, flickering lightning which 'flutters — flutters like a wing — flutters like a broken bird that tries to fly and sinks again and again struggles'. Katherine Mansfield's own favourite image of herself imprisoned by her disease, which began with an image of her lungs as water-wings and shifted into the bird or Pegasus artist-figure with a broken wing, is here applied to the trapped husband. When his moon-wife goes to bed he sits out on the balcony in the moonlight, but not for his own pleasure: 'He gets very cold there, staring at the balcony rail.' She is cold in England, sitting practically in the fire. He is cold in the south, and cannot face the moon.

The suppression of his ego is contrasted with the flowering aloe:

Out of the thick, fleshy leaves of a cactus there rose an

aloe stem loaded with pale flowers that looked as though they had been cut out of butter; light flashed upon the lifted spears of the palms; over a bed of scarlet waxen flowers some big black insects 'zoom-zoomed'; great, gaudy creeper, orange splashed with jet, sprawled against a wall.

The little girls who flee when they catch sight of him are frightened because, unlike his wife, they sense the huge and to them menacing growth which he is holding down.

She thought he looked pale — but wonderfully handsome with that great tropical tree behind him with its long, spiked horns.

The imagery stresses his suppression of everything that is natural to him, from the pleasure of sex to the honesty of normal behaviour.

The final clamp on the man's trap is his wife's devotion, and the hostility of everyone apart from her in and around the *pension*. All the guests contribute to the perspective of which he is the focus. The 'Two Topknots' emphasise the desiccated sameness of the life. The honeymoon couple, creatures of a different moon from the husband's, underline what the man with the corpse-like wife has lost. The American widow with her lapdog parodies the invalid wife with her servant-husband and sexless loyalty. The General and the Countess (and their driver) confirm the alienation already shown in the contemptuous maidservant and the frightened children. All this he has to endure for the sake of his wife's dependency on him.

When Katherine Mansfield sent the story to Murry for publication she no doubt saw it as a corrective to 'The New Husband' and a form of apology for the attack the poem contained. When she mailed her only copy to him on 12 January she expected him to cherish it, and not just for editorial reasons. 'I think there is not a word I would change or that can be changed,' she wrote, 'so would you examine the proofs with the MS?'[16] It was her objective assessment, a perfect piece of art. Murry did not understand. He was at this time drifting into an emotional entanglement in London and was doing what he thought was the agreed thing, house-hunting for a place where Katherine might live in the south of England. A letter he wrote near the end of January shows their cross-purposes.

> You will, I hope, have got the notes which I sent you from Sussex. I came back without having found a house, but with the firm conviction that Sussex is a county of *incomparable* beauty, and that I must try might and main to find something there. I walked 30 miles on Saturday and Sunday. The walk on Sunday was divine. Darling, I'm sure you wouldn't believe what the South Downs can be on their day even in January. There was a bright, pale-blue sky, with tufts of cloud. We were walking on the lower slope of the Downs on the north side. Below us, gently sloping away to the right were miles on miles of the Sussex weald rolling away to the north. The strangest and most wonderful thing about it was the colour — it seemed to be all golden, with dark brown splashes where the woods were, and every now and then a glimmer of vivid green. I can't describe it; it needs patience and art. But it made a profound impression upon me — of wideness and peace, a queer sense that the country instead of being alien wanted to protect and shelter you, almost to lull you into her own richness. I felt that you and I could grow wise and unfretted there, that the note of hysteria would go out of all that I did.[17]

Such open enthusiasm for England was, she must have thought, his egotistical response to her bravely generous and balanced attempt at identifying what his life in exile with her would be for him. Her reaction to his letter was so violent that he cut his gordian knot with *The Athenaeum* and England and made haste to join her in Menton.

'Miss Brill', written soon after Katherine Mansfield arrived in Menton in November 1920, is structurally related to 'Bliss' as a story in which a shift of feeling in one character is conveyed in a single scene. With unity of action, time and place these shorter stories tend to seem more 'realistic' than episodic pieces like _Prelude_ or 'Je ne parle pas français'. However, this smooth narrative texture is in a sense appearance only. As much as in _Prelude_ the stories are structured according to the demands of symbolist patterning and almost every detail has a symbolic as well as narrative context. There are also narrative suppressions and ellipses in stories like 'Miss Brill', though they are less obvious than in the longer stories as they are not signalled by formal divisions in the text.

'Miss Brill' has often been regarded as a moral, even as a sentimental story. It drew letters of thanks from solitary readers, and the author herself seems to have rather basked in such attention, writing to Murry after she had received these letters:

> One writes (_one_ reason why is) because one does care so passionately that one _must_ show it — one must declare one's love.[18]

But in writing the story she adhered to Symbolist principles. Rather than 'declaring her love' she kept her own, or rather the narrator's point of view rigorously out of the story. The events and images function dramatically, the narrator providing only 'objective' description. This is true even of the famous last lines of the story:

> The box that the fur came out of was on the bed. She unclasped the necklet quickly; quickly, without looking, laid it inside. But when she put the lid on she thought she heard something crying.

The narrator provides objective information, then the rapid rhythms of 'quickly; quickly, without looking' shade into the representation of Miss Brill's agitated state. The closing perception of the story is Miss Brill's and not the narrator's and is entirely in accord with her neurotic, fantastic imagination. And it is entirely unsentimental, suggesting very firmly the fear and horror which attend the suppression of any human being.

In 'Miss Brill' all is conveyed obliquely, through concrete imagery and the dramatic device of Miss Brill's inner monologue. Not once is her inner state alluded to or described directly. The story is thus the perfect example of the technique Mansfield described to Murry — oblique, delicately suggestive:

> I might write about a boy eating strawberries or a woman combing her hair on a windy morning and that is the only way I can ever mention [deserts of vast eternity].[19]

The language of the story also reaches a high degree of perfection. She wrote in a well-known letter to Richard Murry that:

> In *Miss Brill* I choose not only the length of every sentence, but even the sound of every sentence. I choose the rise and fall of every paragraph to fit her, and to fit her on that very day at that very moment. After I'd written it I read it aloud — numbers of times — just as one would *play over* a musical composition — trying to get it nearer and nearer the expression of Miss Brill — until it fitted her.[20]

The author's own satisfaction with the style of 'Miss Brill' suggests her success in the story. A poetic intensity and concretion is sustained throughout, the sound of the words and the prose rhythms conveying and enriching meaning. The use of the musical analogy for 'Miss Brill' in the passage quoted above also has more direct relevance. The story is shaped, specifically, as a lament, and something of the quality of a sung lament is deliberately infused into it by the use of para-musical prose rhythms in some sections.

The story is constructed around a series of parallels and contrasts designed to expose with increasing clarity the inner state of the central character. The key themes are the opposition between age and youth, stasis and vitality, solitude and community, illusion and reality.

Miss Brill herself is old, as we realise immediately from the author's handling of her stylised inner monologue. Her speech patterns are those of a nervous, fussy, elderly person. She is associated in the first paragraph of the story with her fur, which acts as a mirror image of the woman herself. The fur, too, is old, with 'dim' eyes, and its nose is 'not at all firm'; 'Never mind — a little dab of black sealing wax when the time came — when it was absolutely necessary . . .' The ellipsis signals Miss Brill's reluctance to recognise a time when 'it' will be absolutely necessary, her avoidance of the thought of decay or decomposition.

In the five and a half pages of the story Miss Brill's state is explored through a series of figures who act as parallels for her. At the Jardins Publiques she sits beside an old couple who are as 'still as statues', and she notices the other regular visitors to the park — 'There was something funny about nearly all of them. They were odd, silent, nearly all old' — though Miss Brill does not, explicitly, include herself in this company. The most extended view which she has of any other visitor to the park is of a single woman in an ermine toque 'bought when her hair was yellow. Now everything, her hair, her face, even her eyes, was the same colour as the shabby ermine, and her hand, in its cleaned glove, lifted to dab her lips, was a tiny yellowish paw.' The woman in the toque parallels Miss Brill in the efforts which she has made to 'touch up' her shabby appearance before entering the park. The link between the furs — dead animals retaining the appearance of life — and the old people, is insisted on. Miss Brill is linked finally to another elderly man to whom she reads the newspaper:

> She had got quite used to the frail head on the cotton pillow, the hollowed eyes, the open mouth and the high pinched nose. If he'd been dead she mightn't have noticed for weeks; she wouldn't have minded.

He too is a moribund figure, retaining little more than the appearance of life.

The pictures of the old are counterpointed by glimpses Miss Brill has of the younger people in the park, who all seem to be much further away. The old people are solitary and motionless. The younger ones are presented as energetic and vigorous — the conductor of the band flaps his arms, the bandsmen blow out their cheeks. Little children 'swoop' and 'laugh', young mothers 'rush', 'high stepping'. Their vitality distinguishes them, as does the fact that they are all in groups or, more relevantly, in pairs:

> Two young girls in red came by and two young soldiers in blue met them, and they laughed and paired and went off arm in arm.

The theme of solitude against community has already been introduced in the second paragraph where Miss Brill ironically sees herself and the other regular visitors to the park as 'the family', as compared with the 'strangers', the seasonal visitors. (The reverse is of course the case: the regular visitors are all strangers — all alone — whereas the visitors are in family groups.) The theme of false community appears again in the scene with the 'ermine toque'. This woman approaches a 'gentleman' and tries to engage him in conversation. As she chatters, he lights a cigarette and 'while she was still talking and laughing, flicked the match away and walked on'. The 'ermine toque's' pitifully inappropriate behaviour and her imaginary sense of relationship anticipate the central moment of the story. The theme of false community is an integral part of Miss Brill's epiphany, as is the theme of the discrepancy between appearance and reality which is also developed through the story.

From the beginning, the things which Miss Brill sees are described in 'stagey' terms. She herself touches up her fur, that is, her appearance, before she sets out for the park. She sees other elderly people as 'statues'; the running little girls are 'dolls'. Towards the end of the story, her vision flowers into explicit recognition. She realises that everything she sees is like a play:

> How she loved sitting here, watching it all! It was like a play. It was exactly like a play. Who could believe the sky at the back wasn't painted? But it wasn't until a little brown dog trotted on solemnly and then slowly trotted off, like a little 'theatre' dog, a little dog that had been drugged, that Miss Brill discovered what it was that made it so exciting. They were all on the stage. They weren't only the audience, not

only looking on; they were acting. Even she had a part and came every Sunday.

When she realises this, Miss Brill looks again at the band, the play within the play. As the music flows out, she has her false epiphany. She feels at one with everyone else, everyone seems united, through the music and also because they are all part of a play and are in this sense a 'company':

> . . . And Miss Brill's eyes filled with tears and she looked smiling at all the other members of the company. Yes, we understand, she thought — though what they understood she didn't know.

The falsity of this sense of community is revealed almost immediately. A young couple replace the silent old couple on the seat beside Miss Brill. They are drawn immediately into her imaginary play — 'The hero and heroine, of course, just arrived from his father's yacht' — only to destroy all its meaning as soon as they actually speak:

> '. . . Why doesn't she keep her silly old mug at home?' 'It's her fu-fur which is so funny . . . It's exactly like a fried whiting.'

Thus it is revealed to Miss Brill in the most painful possible way that her play is a play within her mind only. We are made to see the isolation of each individual within their own consciousness, and the all too common discrepancy between on the one hand the appearance which the mind creates through imagination and memory, and on the other hand reality, in the sense of what is generally agreed to be the truth. Miss Brill's most recent sustaining illusion has been that on her Sunday afternoon visits to the Jardins Publiques she has been part of a community of feeling and interest. She has felt that the part which she plays in the Sunday afternoon pageant has mattered to others as theirs had mattered to her. We know that Miss Brill's existence is barely tolerable, but we also know that she transforms her meagre situation, by the power of her imagination, which is creative. She idealises what she sees around her and idealises herself, revealing herself as an artist in this sense.

The young couple tear down the veil of illusion, leaving Miss Brill with nothing. She realises the cruelty of other human beings in the cruelty and indifference of the young couple — whom *she* has idealised. She has hoped that if she were to miss a Sunday afternoon (for reasons not admitted to consciousness) she would in her turn be missed. It is now apparent that this is doubtful, and that certainly no one would care. And Miss Brill realises finally that she does not appear to others as she does to herself (she does not see her face as a 'silly old mug').

Miss Brill's epiphany is too unbearable and her new knowledge cannot be admitted to consciousness at this moment. Hence the ellipsis which follows the speech of the young couple. Miss Brill does not think about what she has just realised, though it may make its way back into consciousness by degrees. But, we sense, she will then transform this knowledge too by the power of her imagination, the saving grace of her life. This is suggested through the coda of the story as she puts her fur away, thus showing her ability to adjust and construct new appearances.

Miss Brill's situation is extreme and her isolation is intensified because she is a spinster abroad in a foreign country. Yet in Mansfield's view we are all ultimately solitary, and human beings are fundamentally cruel and indifferent to one another except in the rare instances where they love. Without love, and without the comfort of illusions, the reality of life can be grim indeed. 'Miss Brill', for all its brevity, presents a genuinely tragic view of experience. The central character lacks love and has only her capacity of creative imagination between herself and the void. She will go on living and transforming her experience into tolerable forms, but the value and meaning of life on this level is questionable. Without love, what other 'real ideal' can enter Miss Brill's life? The brief descriptions of natural beauty — the sea, the golden leaves, the blue sky — suggest one possibility, but these are the perceptions of the narrator, and are introduced as thematic motifs, rather than being important to Miss Brill. Through a combination of character and circumstance, Miss

Brill's life has been reduced to the barest minimum necessary to continued existence. The story is a radical questioning of the meaning of such existence, and of the purpose of the life-force which makes her carry on on these terms.

'Poison' was written at about the same time as 'Miss Brill', in November 1920, but as Katherine Mansfield explained in a letter to Murry it was 'quite a different kind' of work. According to Murry, it was omitted from *The Garden Party* because he thought it 'not wholly successful', and in a reply to him the author herself concluded 'I suppose I haven't brought it off in *Poison*'. The story seems slight at first reading, even confused, and the poison motif in particular seems inadequately worked out. Set beside her outline of what she wanted to create, the finished story seems distinctly flimsy. It provoked one of her longest commentaries:

> The story is told by (evidently) a worldly, rather cynical (not wholly cynical) man *against* himself (but not altogether) when he was so absurdly young. You know how young by his idea of what woman is. She has been up to now, only the vision, only she who passes. You realise that? And here he has put *all* his passion into this Beatrice. It's *promiscuous love*, not understood as such by him; perfectly understood as such by her. But you realise, the *vie de luxe* they are living — the very table — sweets, liqueurs, lilies, pearls. And you realise? she expects a letter from someone calling her away. *Fully* expects it? That accounts for her farewell AND her declaration. And when it doesn't come even her *commonness* peeps out — the newspaper touch of such a woman. She can't disguise her chagrin. She gives herself away . . . He, of course, laughs at it now, and laughs at her. Take what he says about her 'sense of order' and the crocodile. But he also regrets the self who dead privately would have been young enough to have actually wanted to *marry* such a woman. But I meant it to be light — tossed off — and yet through it — oh, subtly — the lament for youthful belief. These are the rapid confessions one receives sometimes from a glove or a cigarette or a hat.

I suppose I haven't brought it off in *Poison*. It wanted a light, light hand — and then with that newspaper a sudden . . . let me see, *lowering* of it all — just what happens in promiscuous love after passion. A glimpse of staleness. And the story is told by the man who gives himself away and hides his traces at the same moment.[21]

Why is it that the author doesn't succeed in conveying all this? There seem to be two main reasons. One lies in the first-person narration by a male character, Katherine Mansfield's second attempt after 'Je ne parle pas français'. The success of the latter story depended, however, on the sharply realised character of Raoul Duquette. In 'Poison', the author doesn't seem to have had a sufficiently clear idea of her central character. Though he was to be 'worldly, rather cynical (not wholly cynical)' this is as far as the outline goes, and a problem with the identity of the narrator subsequently makes itself felt throughout the story of which he is both teller and subject.

Because the narrator's present character is not clearly established through tone or imagery, the excursions into the past and explorations of his former self do not quite succeed. We are unable to discriminate between past and present or to measure change, and so the central theme, the 'lament for youthful belief', is lost. This uncertainty over the narrator disrupts the formal texture of the story to the extent that in some passages we are not even sure that it is the narrator who is speaking: the perceptions and vocabulary seem to float free of the supposed narrative context:

'Who are you?' Who was she? She was — Woman.

. . . On the first warm evening in spring, when lights shone like pearls through the lilac air and voices murmured in the fresh-flowering gardens, it was she who sang in the tall house with the tulle curtains. As one drove in the moonlight through the foreign city hers was the shadow that fell across the quivering gold of the shutters. When the lamp was lighted, in the new-born stillness her steps passed your door . . .

The other major source of weakness in the story seems to lie in lack of control over imagery. By comparison with the sharp use of detail for symbolic purpose in 'Bliss' and 'Miss Brill', the structure of 'Poison' seems loose and indiscriminate. To take a specific example: rather than using one central image for 'promiscuous love', such as the lily, which has neat and appropriate overtones,[22] the author provides a wealth of alternative detail — pearls, freesias, figs, sweets — which merely confuses and distracts the reader. There is a loss in sharpness of focus and in consequence no clear sense of a direction for interpretation. The technique of repeated imagery is little used in this story, which confirms our impression that it is not clearly articulated or organised as a whole. And imagery is not firmly linked to character and emotional tone. For example, the analogy between the 'newspaper world' and Beatrice's 'commonness', alluded to in the letter to Murry, is not made clear at the critical moment when Beatrice tears off the newspaper wrapper. Thus the intended effect of a sudden 'lowering of it all' is simply not communicated to the reader.

The letter to Murry indicates her intention to use in 'Poison' an oblique, symbolist method, to convey her themes by means of objective correlatives — 'these are the rapid confessions one receives sometimes from a glove or a cigarette or a hat'. Judged in these terms, and against the standard of stories like 'Miss Brill' which use the same technique, 'Poison' is a relative failure. Yet it has certain qualities, especially a kind of alternative structure which in a sense works against the symbolic one. This is worth exploration, for it points forward to some of the later writing, for example in 'A Married Man's Story'. Both 'Poison' and 'A Married Man's Story' are concerned with the relationship between truth and language. 'Poison' shows a repeated awareness of a discrepancy between the two. From the start, the two lovers are shown to be deceiving each other. Beatrice first claims an indifference to the internal arrangement and décor of her room which she does not feel. She also suggested to the narrator that there is no need for her to wear a wedding ring (no need to pretend), and he paradoxically agrees with her though he feels internally the exact opposite — he wishes for a large, solid and fashionable church-wedding to nail down his Beatrice. One of the key passages of the story, Beatrice's declaration of love, is weighted with this kind of ambiguity. It is a lie, in effect, yet it never quite lies, for there are always redeeming phrases — 'not really', 'I believe':

> I put my arm round her. 'Then you wouldn't fly away?'
> And she said rapidly and softly: 'No! No! Not for worlds. Not really. I love this place. I've loved being here. I could stay here for years, I believe. I've never been so happy as I have these last two months, and you've been so perfect to me, dearest, in every way.'

At one point in the story the narrator says categorically that he 'knows' something — he knows that Beatrice is his. The very fact that he claims to know something rouses our suspicions, especially in the context of the absent letter which is an ever present element in the story (the first sentence runs: 'The post was very late'). This letter is given some sort of identity for the reader fairly early on as the narrator speaks of the impossible third at the luncheon table:

> As always, the sight of the table laid for two — for two people only — and yet so finished, so perfect, there was no possible room for a third, gave me a queer, quick thrill . . .

This is a still life, an artificial arrangement, which is doomed to be destroyed exactly like Bertha's dinner party arrangement in 'Bliss'. The narrator is brought to awareness of the truth about the letter through action and situation rather than through speech. He shrugs off Beatrice's spoken rudeness to him on at least two occasions, first when he comes to tell her there are no letters, and later when she remarks scornfully that he 'wouldn't hurt a fly'. But her chagrin about the non-arrival of the letter gradually makes itself felt through attitude and gesture, combined with her repeated enquiries about the mail. Her obsession causes the narrator to realise the existence of the letter. Simultaneously, he realises its content, for he does not need to read the letter to know what it means for him. It means exactly the same thing whether it is a summons for Beatrice or a rebuff, because it reveals the extent of her indifference and duplicity towards him.

Thus it is through situation and the structure of communication (the letter's place as an object in a line of communication) that the truth is realised, not through language as such. For the letter is 'empty' (unread), and this is important in the context of the story's play on the unreliability of language. The narrator's realisation of the truth coincides necessarily with his realisation of this unreliability: the two realisations must be interdependent for him:

> But I lifted my glass and drank, sipped rather — sipped slowly, deliberately, looking at that dark head and thinking of — postmen and blue beetles and farewells that were not farewells and . . .
> Good God! Was it fancy? No, it wasn't fancy. The drink tasted chill, bitter, *queer*.

Situation and underlying structures are more solid touchstones of reality than language-in-operation. There is a suggestion in 'Poison' that language is especially unreliable as a medium because it is common currency. It is open to use and abuse for all the purposes of everyday life, and is associated with such sordid activities as, for example, the newspaper reporting of a poison trial:

> But quickly she tossed the paper away on to the stone.
> 'There's nothing in it,' said she. 'Nothing. There's only some poison trial. Either some man did or didn't murder his wife, and twenty thousand people have sat in court every day and two million words have been wired all over the world after each proceeding.'

This question is not pursued here, but is taken up again in 'A Married Man's Story', where Katherine Mansfield addresses herself to a complex of related problems involving the independence and materiality of language:

That about the wolves won't do. Curious! Before I wrote it down, while it was still in my head, I was delighted with it. It seemed to express, and more, to suggest, just what I wanted to say. But written, I can smell the falseness immediately, and the . . . source of the smell is in that word fleet. Don't you agree? Fleet, grey brothers! 'Fleet'. A word I never use. When I wrote 'wolves' it skimmed across my mind like a shadow and I couldn't resist it. Tell me! Tell me! Why is it so difficult to write simply — and not simply only but *sotto voce*, if you know what I mean? That is how I long to write. No fine effects — no bravura. But just the plain truth, as only a liar can tell it.[23]

It is a characteristic of these first-person narratives that they are preoccupied with the possibilities and limitations of expression in prose. This may be because in such narratives there is no easy, conventional relationship between reader and writer, as there is in third-person narrative. 'Poison', existing like 'A Married Man's Story' and 'The Canary' on the boundaries of expression, is worth reading for this exploratory quality alone, if not for the more conventional reasons adduced by Murry in his introduction to *Something Childish, and Other Stories*: 'I have now changed my mind: it now seems to me a little masterpiece,' he wrote.

'The Daughters of the Late Colonel' was written in Menton on 13 December 1920. Ida Baker was present, ministering, and records the occasion:

I remember the night she finished *The Daughters of the Late Colonel*, that gentle caricature of her cousin Sylvia Payne and me, which she wrote in about three or four hours with hardly a break or correction. 'It's finished! It's finished!' she called. 'Celebration with tea!'[24]

In February 1922, after a year of splendid creativity had followed, she could still call it one of her favourites. To William Gerhardi she wrote,

The only story that satisfies me to any extent is the one you
understand so well, *The Daughters of the Late Col.*, and parts
of *Je ne parle pas*.[25]

What she seems to have had in mind when she recorded that
opinion was its technical brilliance rather than its subject matter.
In a letter to Richard Murry, written only a few weeks after the
story was put on paper, she told him,

> I have written a huge long story of a rather new kind. It's the
> outcome of the *Prelude* method — it just unfolds and opens
> — But I hope it's an advance on *Prelude*. In fact, I know it's
> that because the technique is stronger.[26]

Her own affection for the story carries weight. It is technically
one of the most sophisticated stories she wrote, and she knew
how very much more than Ida's 'gentle caricature' her technique
made it.

The style she adopts is interior monologue externalised by the
use of the third person, which allows continual shifts of focus,
from the Daughters in concert, to their separate trains of thought,
and into the author's own discreetly distancing comments. In the
opening of the final section, for instance, the interior perspective
is chiefly Josephine's, but it modulates from inside to outside,
never quite detaching itself from Josephine while permitting only
the faintest subjective bias to the outside happenings, the barrel-
organ, the sunlight, and finally the music again.

> But at that moment in the street below a barrel-organ struck
> up. Josephine and Constantia sprang to their feet together.
>   'Run, Con,' said Josephine. 'Run quickly. There's sixpence
> on the —'
>   Then they remembered. It didn't matter. They would never
> have to stop the organ-grinder again. Never again would she
> and Constantia be told to make that monkey take his noise
> somewhere else. Never would sound that loud, strange bellow
> when father thought they were not hurrying enough. The
> organ-grinder might play there all day and the stick would
> not thump.

It never will thump again,
It never will thump again,
played the barrel-organ.

What was Constantia thinking? She had such a strange smile, she looked different. She couldn't be going to cry.

'Jug, Jug,' said Constantia softly, pressing her hands together. 'Do you know what day it is? It's Saturday. It's a week today, a whole week.'

A week since father died,
A week since father died,
cried the barrel-organ. And Josephine, too, forgot to be practical and sensible; she smiled faintly, strangely. On the Indian carpet there fell a square of sunlight, pale red; it came and went and came — and stayed, deepened — until it shone almost golden.

'The sun's out,' said Josephine, as though it really mattered.

A perfect fountain of bubbling notes shook from the barrel-organ, round, bright notes, carelessly scattered.

Even the Colonel is present here, in the phrase 'make that monkey take his noise somewhere else'. The author slips in with 'And Josephine, too, forgot', but the adjectives which follow are rather Josephine's than the author's, her conscious pose, so that we are immediately back inside her. When the sunshine penetrates the room we hear Josephine's thought, 'as though it really mattered', at the same time as we hear the author hinting at a judgement and at the conclusion of the story. The sunshine matters, and yet it will signal no real change. Every word here is luminous with implication.

Structurally, too, it is a sophistication of the *Prelude* method. It 'unfolds' like *Prelude* through twelve sections or scenes, but with an even more functional appropriateness than the earlier story. Like *Prelude* each section develops by a seemingly random association of ideas from its predecessor, but more functionally because the randomness directly imitates the random thought-processes of the Daughters. Section III shifts into Section IV, for instance, via the memory of father opening only the one distinctly glaring eye before he died, into the difficulty which the memory of that sight created when the vicar conventionally enquired whether the Colonel's end had been peaceful.

> It had made it very awkward for them when Mr Farolles, of St John's, called the same afternoon.
>
> 'The end was quite peaceful, I trust?' were the first words he said as he glided towards them through the dark drawing-room.
>
> 'Quite,' said Josephine faintly. They both hung their heads. Both of them felt certain that eye wasn't at all a peaceful eye.

The inconsequential sequence covers, by the end, all the revelatory incidents which have followed the Colonel's death. Their inconsequentiality accurately reflects the waywardness of the Daughters' thinking and the way events impinge on them from unforeseeable directions.

The structure of the twelve scenes, however, is anything but inconsequential. It falls into two halves, the second six scenes repeating the pattern of the first six exactly. Nurse Andrews dominates the second and third scenes of the first half, while Cyril dominates the second and third scenes of the second half. Mr Farolles confronts the Daughters in the fourth scene of the first half, and they try to confront Kate in the fourth scene of the second half. The fifth scene of the first half is entirely Josephine's, while the fifth scene of the second half is entirely Constantia's. Both opening scenes in each half show them together, with a brief separate thought from each of them, and both of the concluding scenes, the sixth and the twelfth, begin with the two of them considered jointly and then alternately. The sixth gives us Jug and Con together, then Jug alone, then Con alone, and finally Jug. The twelfth gives us Jug and Con together, followed by Jug alone, then Con, then Jug, then Con, and ends with the two of them together again. This hidden organisation of the seemingly inconsequential is in its way an accurate image of Katherine Mansfield's presentation of the sisters. The wayward surface appearance of their actions, like the ripples of wind on water, conceals a powerful current which sweeps them directly on to their fate, the remainder of their timorous and sunless existence.

The effect of the wayward scenes is of course cumulative. The first half, which deals with the events of the week following the Colonel's death, is like a door slowly opening. The second, which is chiefly set at the end of the week, sees it close again. The first half has an ascending scale of victimisers, from Nurse Andrews, through Kate to the Colonel himself, the prime mover of the victimisations. It ends in the sixth section with Constantia's triumphant assertion of the freedom to be weak.

> 'Why shouldn't we be weak for once in our lives, Jug? It's quite excusable. Let's be weak — be weak, Jug. It's much nicer to be weak than to be strong.'
>   And then she did one of those amazingly bold things that she'd done about twice before in their lives; she marched over to the wardrobe, turned the key, and took it out of the lock. Took it out of the lock and held it up to Josephine, showing Josephine by her extraordinary smile that she knew what she'd done, she'd risked deliberately father being in there among his overcoats.

The second half brings in the different perspective of Cyril, the nephew equally intimidated by the Colonel and by his Daughters. Cyril's aunts in their auntishness hint at some of the Colonel's legacies, while at the same time making a contrast with the temporary nature of the embarrassment that Cyril suffers in front of the Colonel. Cyril's eagerness to escape makes the feminist point about the Daughters being caught in the Colonel's trap, in preparation for the full recognition of the trap which emerges via the problem of Kate in the final scene of the story.

Kate with her noise and her insistence on decisions ('Fried or boiled?') is the Colonel's most malign legacy. To dismiss her, to make that decision, would mean the Daughters rejecting all the inheritance of their old maid roles. Kate's 'bouncing' is like the Colonel's stick-thumping, or Nurse Andrews with her clock-watching, or the barrel-organ's music bursting out, manifestations of energy which they have come to associate with terror. The Colonel's noise-making instrument, his thumping stick, is also an emblem of his helplessness, but the Daughters have inherited too much terror to know that. They live in continual fear of things bursting out of confined spaces — including the Colonel himself out of his cupboards and drawers — and so cannot see the confined space in which they too are trapped as anything but a protection.[27]

The trap, the predetermined fate of the Daughters, is suggested through Katherine Mansfield's stock symbol of life, the sun. Josephine, the more 'practical and sensible' of the sisters, is sun and Constantia is moon. In the final scene the sun intrudes its light on their consideration of the new pattern offered them by life now that the Colonel is dead.

> The sunlight pressed through the windows, thieved its way in, flashed its light over the furniture and the photographs. Josephine watched it. When it came to mother's photograph, the enlargement over the piano, it lingered as though puzzled to find so little remained of mother, except the ear-rings shaped like tiny pagodas and a black feather boa.

Josephine thinks over their past life and its fragile cargo of lost opportunities.

> . . . And that was all. The rest had been looking after father, and at the same time keeping out of father's way. But now? But now? The thieving sun touched Josephine gently. She lifted her face. She was drawn over to the window by gentle beams . . .

Attention then turns to moon-like Constantia and her even more vague sense of deprivation. They turn to one another with the same question, and with the same inabilities:

> They stopped; they waited for each other.
>
> 'Go on Con,' said Josephine.
>
> 'No, no, Jug; after you,' said Constantia.
>
> A pause. Then Constantia said faintly, 'I can't say what I was going to say, Jug, because I've forgotten what it was . . . that I was going to say.'

> Josephine was silent for a moment. She stared at a big cloud where the sun had been. Then she replied shortly, 'I've forgotten too.'

Constantia's amazing boldness has gone, and she dare not follow her train of thought. Josephine has to follow down the same cul-de-sac. They cannot face the outflow of energy that would mean their release from confinement. This is the point to which their week of adjustment has taken them, and it is the end of their adjustment. The rest of their lives is predetermined. The sun, weirdly foreshadowed by the one eye glaring from the dying Colonel's purple face, has followed the ogre to his grave.

> Oh, what a difference it would have made, what a difference to their memory of him, how much easier to tell people about it, if he had only opened both! But no — one eye only. It glared at them a moment and then . . . went out.

The Daughters' clouds are grey, not purple, but their sun expires in the same way. They are the Colonel's too-late Daughters.

In a letter to Gerhardi of June 1921 Katherine Mansfield registered her distress at the callow way in which the story had been read. She did acknowledge that the response it calls for is a difficult feat of balance. 'While I was writing it,' she told Gerhardi,

> I lived for it but when it was finished, I confess I hoped very much that my readers would understand what I was trying to express. But very few did. They thought it was 'cruel'; they thought I was 'sneering' at Jug and Constantia; or they thought it was 'drab'. And in the last paragraph I was 'poking fun at the poor old things.'[28]

The response must be as deliberately exact as the story. The balancing act is needed because the pathos so precisely matches the comedy, and the comic old maids are helpless in their everlasting trap. Out of the comedy and framed by the trap emerges the beauty of which they can know nothing, except for the door which momentarily opens to Constantia on her announcement that 'It's much nicer to be weak than to be strong.' The letter to Gerhardi continues:

> It's almost terrifying to be so misunderstood. There was a moment when I first had 'the idea' when I saw the two sisters as *amusing*; but the moment I looked deeper (let me be quite frank) I bowed down to the beauty that was hidden in their lives and to discover that was all my desire . . . All was meant, of course, to lead up to that last paragraph, when my two flowerless ones turned with that timid gesture, to the sun. 'Perhaps *now* . . .' And after that, it seemed to me, they died as surely as Father was dead . . .

If we have to see Carco in Raoul Duquette and Murry in Robert Salesby, we should also register in Constantia the tribute to Ida Baker, in whose company the story was set down, as a comparably scrupulous portrait with an incomparably more far-reaching frame of reference. Duquette is a portrait of a poseur, Robert Salesby a man castrated by a highly specific trap. The trap the Daughters are in is deeper, more basic, in a social perspective which reaches far beyond the bounds of their capacity to recognise it. And the telling of their story, that supremely delicate feat of balance and subtly allusive images, fully justifies the accolade David Daiches[29] gave it, as a landmark in the history of the short story.

4 The stories 1921-22: Sierre and Paris

Katherine Mansfield died in the Gurdjieff Institute on 9 January 1923. She gave up writing and made her will the previous August, and joined Gurdjieff in October. The Institute was her final and most unlikely attempt to find a cure for the disease which had been riding her more and more heavily since 1918. In March 1921 she finally abandoned England, and the Hampstead house in which the Murrys had lived intermittently since August 1918 was sold. Tuberculosis now dictated mountain air, and in May 1921 she went to a hotel in Switzerland with Ida Baker. Murry joined her at the Chalet les Sapins in the mountains near Montana-sur-Sierre in July. The months that followed allowed her to produce the great New Zealand stories. Then in January 1922, driven on by her disease, she went to Paris with the ever-loyal Ida for a final try at a medical cure. The more desperate she became the more unreal the cures she tried. When this last and most quackish of the medical cures had obviously failed, by the autumn of 1922, she retreated to the spiritualism of Gurdjieff. That did not last her long either.

During the two relatively settled phases of these last years, in the Swiss Alps and for a month or two in Paris, there was the isolation and the occasion necessary for her best writing. She was terrified of death, and terrified that it would catch her before she had set down what she felt was still in her. Mostly her mind was on the New Zealand of her youth, and the urge to create her vision of it as a memorial to her dead brother never quite left her. The last stories are deeply engaged with death, though in the form of encounters with the death of others rather than her own.

'The Voyage' was written at the Chalet les Sapins in August 1921,[1] early in the experimental phase which led up to that period of intense creativity which produced 'At the Bay', 'The

Garden-Party' and 'The Doll's House' in September and October 1921. New Zealand subjects occupied her mind throughout this period. They provide half the stories of *The Garden-Party*, the volume published in 1922, and were to have provided two-thirds of the next volume, *The Doves' Nest*, which Murry issued in 1923 after Katherine Mansfield's death. For that volume she planned to have six stories about New Zealand and three about London. In the event only four were written, all of them New Zealand stories.

'The Voyage' has many features in common with the Burnell and Sheridan cycles, which were to be largely written in the succeeding months, but it is a wholly distinct entity. It has the child's-eye-view of 'At the Bay' and the crystal-clear detailing of 'The Garden-Party', and yet it did not grow out of the auto-biographical substructure of the two story cycles. It has if anything an even greater intensity, because it is freed by its fictional setting from the necessary randomness of the *Karori* cycle and the Sheridan stories. It is complete, with no links outside to other stories or other episodes in the patterns of discovery and growth which make up the Burnell and Sheridan cycles. The whole life of the girl in the story is concentrated into the one experience. 'It wasn't the memory of a real experience. It was a kind of *possession*,' Katherine Mansfield told Gerhardi. Intensely imagined, and complete as it is, it forms the total possession of a total experience. Its completeness has rightly made it one of the most frequently anthologised of all the stories.

It begins on the Wellington docks where the ferry for Picton is waiting, in the dark of an urban and industrial setting.

> It was dark on the Old Wharf, very dark; the wool sheds, the cattle trucks, the cranes standing up so high, the little squat railway engine, all seemed carved out of solid darkness.

It is full of strangers hurrying through the obscurity to the ferry. By contrast the wharf in the Marlborough Sounds on the other side of Cook Strait is bright, tiny, and almost empty of life.

> And now the landing-stage came out to meet them. Slowly

it swam towards the Picton boat, and a man holding a coil of rope, and a cart with a small drooping horse and another man sitting on the step, came too.

Here the houses, like the horses, are 'little'; the cart is 'little', and the path up to grandma's house is 'little'. Only the bed in the centre of the little house where grandpa lies 'like a very old wide-awake bird' is large; that and the framed text enjoining everyone to make the most of the present moment. Her voyage takes Fenella from the adult size and bustle of the capital into the child-sized world of her grandparents. It is a journey from fear to security.

In Wellington, hurrying with her nervous father to the ferry, Fenella is made to feel small and afraid. She is symbolised by the lights of the wharf.

> Here and there on a rounded wood-pile, that was like the stalk of a huge black mushroom, there hung a lantern, but it seemed afraid to unfurl its timid, quivering light in all that blackness; it burned softly, as if for itself.

The hurrying adults, the father's taciturn manner, grandma's anxiety for him to get off the ship before the gangway was taken away, and then her breakdown into tears, all intensify Fenella's fear without allowing her to share in the activity. She does not recognise the adult distress, but suffers her own private oppression. When grandma sobs, it

> was so awful that Fenella quickly turned her back on them, swallowed once, twice, and frowned terribly at a little green star on a mast head.

She is shielded from direct grief over her mother's death yet fearfully conscious of its present impact on the adults.

Reassurance comes when the ferry is under way, and new impressions begin to occupy her mind. The same effect, strangely, appears in her grandmother: 'To her relief grandma seemed no longer sad.' She turns to the present and the business of finding their cabin and restoring the familiar patterns of life. And normality slowly begins to establish itself with Fenella too. She voyages into strange but increasingly secure surroundings.

The story is grounded on this contrast between the dark, dangerous Wellington wharf and the warm stillness of the 'little' township where grandpa is still in bed when they arrive and nothing seems in the least menacing.

> On the table a white cat, that had been folded up like a camel, rose, stretched itself, yawned, and then sprang on to the tips of its toes. Fenella buried one cold little hand in the white, warm fur, and smiled timidly while she stroked and listened to grandma's gentle voice and the rolling tones of grandpa.

She still only stands alongside her shepherds, watching and listening to the present, and registering the adult tones. But the transformation is total, from the huge dark strangeness of the city to the early morning brightness of the township, from the oppressive tension of father, preoccupied and therefore frightening, to grandma's reassuring calm, from night to day. Grandma's umbrella pecks with its swan's head at Fenella's shoulder as they hurry to the ferry. On the voyage it has to be watched and guarded. In grandma's home she can finally lay it to rest:

> Fenella smiled again, and crooked the swan neck over the bed-rail.

It symbolises the answer to the question that came to her mind when she woke: 'Oh, it had all been so sad lately. Was it going to change?' She accepts the present moment as the large black text on grandpa's wall insists, and like the swan-headed umbrella she settles confidently into her home.

The basic contrast between the two ends of the voyage is overlaid with these other patterns. Grandma is first reassuring and then home to Fenella because Fenella's mind dwells intensely in the present, and so does grandma. Fenella is alienated from her father by his distraction, his memory of the past, his wife's death which Fenella cannot share, and of the future, including the need to have Fenella looked after in his parents' home for an indefinite period. Fenella lives too much in the present to have a real sense of how deeply she wants change from the menacing darkness to the bright smallness of grandma's home. There is nothing precious to her in Wellington, and she takes away nothing but a 'neat sausage' of clothing. Her concern is all for grandma's talismanic umbrella. So the world changes with her from the dark to the light, and the new present becomes the idyllic world seen in the opening of 'At the Bay'.

'At the Bay' was written over a period of about six weeks during August and September 1921. It is constructed like 'The Daughters of the Late Colonel' and *Prelude* as a sequence of twelve linked episodes, in each of which indirect free form is used to explore the consciousness of one or more of the central characters. Unlike the other two stories, it has a controlling narrative framework which functions thematically as a means by which the major images of the story are underscored and drawn together. The framing device is the description of the passage of a single day from dawn to dusk, the same frame employed by Virginia Woolf in *The Waves*. In *The Waves* she counterpoints her description of the passage of a man's life with a description of the passage of a single day. Two characteristically Modernist assumptions are conflated: man's life is no more than a single day, a flickering brief candle in the wider context of historical time; but, conversely, the whole of a man's life can be revealed during the course of a single day, even in one epiphanic moment.

In 'At the Bay' the framework of the passing day is employed to deepen the resonances of the story and make transparent the universal references of the particular events described. Jonathan Trout underlines the intention of the technique within the story as he ponders the meaning of his life:

> 'And all the while I am thinking, like that moth, or that butterfly, or whatever it is, "The shortness of life! The shortness of life!" I've only one night or one day, and there's this vast dangerous garden, waiting out there, undiscovered, unexplored.'

The use of a cyclical framework is especially apt here, for the story is concerned with acceptance of the cycles of life and death, in contrast with the earlier *Prelude* where the dominant theme is one of discovery and opening out. The balance of attention has shifted from young Kezia's expanding world to the strained experience of the adults. This shift is reflected in the structure: in 'At the Bay' only two episodes are given to the children, as opposed to five in *Prelude*.

As the day of the story unfolds, a basic dichotomy is established. We see that both the very young and the very old live exclusively in the present. Like Fenella and her grandmother in 'The Voyage', Kezia and her grandmother lose the question of death through their absorption in the physical present:

> 'Say never, say never, say never,' gurgled Kezia, while they lay there laughing in each other's arms. 'Come, that's enough, my squirrel! That's enough, my wild pony!' said old Mrs Fairfield, setting her cap straight. 'Pick up my knitting.'
>
> Both of them had forgotten what the 'never' was about.

The adults are caught uneasily between these two complementary states of absorption and acceptance. They are always under stress exactly because they look continually to the future, hoping for achievement and fulfilment which are continually deferred. All feel that they have been denied in some way, that they have 'missed it', with the exception perhaps of Linda, who sees on this day at least 'something infinitely joyful and loving' in the apocalyptic beams of the setting sun.

The imagery of the story also works through oppositions, which indicate that equilibrium and acceptance are the goal of the story as of its characters. One fundamental opposition is between earth and sea. The sea threatens equilibrium. It is an unstable, subversive element which suggests annihilation and loss of the self, while at the same time it possesses a mysterious and seductive charm. The effort of the women of the story is to remain on the earth, on *terra firma*, and to keep the children from going in too far. Only Beryl flirts with the sea, as she does later with Harry Kember: 'Beryl stood, her arms outstretched, gazing out, and as each wave came she gave the slightest little jump.' But she is undermined by her excursion into the sea ('[she] felt that she was being poisoned'), and rather similarly neither Stanley nor Jonathan can keep a firm control over their early morning bathe. Stanley's bathe is too brief, for he flounces off as soon as Jonathan appears, finding he cannot dominate the sea and have it all to himself. Jonathan stays in too long, and comes out feeling ill, having yielded, as in all his life, too much: 'He ached all over; it was as though someone was wringing the blood out of him.' The land represents control over one's life; the sea represents a yielding to mystery and incalculability which can lead to an undesirable loss of self-determination.

The opposition between day and night is less stark. On one level, the contrast is between the natural, open and 'above-board' (Linda's sun-drenched encounter with her son) and the unnatural and perverse (Beryl's night-time actions and desires). Yet the starkness of this opposition is defused by the introduction of more subtle Biblical allusions which add further depth and extend the meaning of the imagery. Thus the passage from dawn to dusk suggests in 'At the Bay' man's journey from prelapsarian innocence (the first person to appear on the scene at dawn is, we note, the shepherd); to the fall, with the introduction of sexual difference and conflict (in all the scenes between Stanley and his household of women); to intimations of redemption in the scene between Linda and Jonathan (which is in some sense a reckoning); then back to a major source of discord in the sexual encounter between Beryl and Harry Kember. The movement is here again cyclical: the human task is to find equilibrium, balance and proper control. The primacy of this need is affirmed in the final paragraph.

> A cloud, small, serene, floated across the moon. In that moment of darkness the sea sounded deep, troubled. Then the cloud sailed away, and the sound of the sea was a vague murmur, as though it waked out of a dark dream. All was still.

The difficult antithesis between male and female worlds which is presented in such a painfully comic mode in 'The Daughters of

the Late Colonel' appears also in 'At the Bay'. Just as the Colonel
had his thumping stick, the emblem of patriarchal and male
power, so Stanley Burnell hounds his women through the house
in quest of *his* stick, which he is convinced they have hidden from
him deliberately. Like the Colonel, and like Cyril, Stanley is
linked closely with 'mechanical time'. The men of Katherine
Mansfield's stories are all clock-watchers. It is this which ties
them firmly to the objective external world and which makes
them capable of action. As the author is quick to indicate, their
activity provides the necessary support for the women's more
passive dream-world:

> Yes, the coach was there waiting, and Beryl, leaning over the
> open gate, was laughing up at somebody or other just as if
> nothing had happened. The heartlessness of women! The way
> they took it for granted it was your job to slave away for them
> while they didn't even take the trouble to see that your
> walking stick wasn't lost.

The women live by 'real time'.[2] They are vague about the
objective world, living in a subjective state in which time is
measured only by what it gives. Linda Burnell dreams a whole
morning away before she experiences a moment which expands
to draw into itself months, years of experience.

Male and female worlds are interdependent, but the protected
women have, to adopt the commercial imagery of the stories
themselves, the best of the bargain. The less 'developed' male may
be less able to cope with emotional crisis, like Mr Hammond in
'The Stranger' for example, whose inability to bear a deviation
from clock time in the opening pages of the story portends his
later breakdown.

A further and related theme which is carried over from 'The
Daughters of the Late Colonel' is a distinction between true and
false (or mechanical) memory. Mechanical memory works by rote,
by date, by the clock: it is symbolised in 'The Daughters' by the
Colonel's photograph of his dead wife:

> The sunlight pressed through the windows, thieved its way in,

flashed its light over the furniture and the photographs. Josephine watched it. When it came to mother's photograph, the enlargement over the piano, it lingered as though puzzled to find so little remained of mother, except the ear-rings shaped like tiny pagodas and a black feather boa. Why did the photographs of dead people always fade so? wondered Josephine. As soon as a person was dead their photograph died too.

By contrast with their father, the daughters have 'real', organic memory, from which, in their case, there can be no escape: the past dominates the present, leaving no way open for the future.

In 'At the Bay', mechanical memory is epitomised in Mrs Stubbs' photographs of her dead husband. In the scene in which she 'seduces' Alice, much as Mrs Kember seduces Beryl, her apparently pious memory of her husband, of whom she has large and numerous photographs, is belied by her broad hint to the girl:

'All the same, my dear,' she said surprisingly, 'freedom's best!' Her soft, fat chuckle sounded like a purr. 'Freedom's best,' said Mrs Stubbs again.

Freedom! Alice gave a loud, silly little titter. She felt awkward. Her mind flew back to her own kitching. Ever so queer! She wanted to be back in it again.

Linda and her mother share the Daughters' organic memory, and their ability to plunge easily back into the past, to recreate the very feel and texture of experience:

. . . Now she sat on the veranda of their Tasmanian home, leaning against her father's knee. And he promised, 'As soon as you and I are old enough, Linny, we'll cut off somewhere, we'll escape. Two boys together. I have a fancy I'd like to sail up a river in China.' Linda saw that river, very wide, covered with little rafts and boats. She saw the yellow hats of the boatmen and she heard their high, thin voices as they called . . .

'Yes, papa,'

But just then a very broad young man with bright ginger hair walked slowly past their house, and slowly, solemnly even, uncovered . . .

But, unlike the Daughters, they are able to *judge* the past and to compare and contrast it with present experience. Thus, in Katherine Mansfield's own words, they can become free of it and make it their servant rather than their master.[3] Mrs Fairfield presents this process at its most complete:

It was the old woman's turn to consider. Did it make her sad? To look back, back. To stare down the years, as Kezia had seen her doing. To look after *them* as a woman does, long after *they* were out of sight. Did it make her sad? No, life was like that.

As the 'thoughts' of the characters interpenetrate and cut across one another the author is able to suggest the opacity of human character, and the difficulty of communication as 'the mists rise and fall'. A very obvious example is the misunderstanding between Jonathan Trout and Stanley Burnell in the early morning bathing scene. There is also the ironically pointed hostility between Beryl and the servant, Alice. Anxious to avoid recognition of the parallel between her own position in life and that of Alice, Beryl continually abuses and misunderstands her. As Alice goes out for her afternoon off,

Beryl, sitting in the window, fanning her freshly washed hair, thought she had never seen such a guy . . . She supposed Alice had picked up some horrible common larrikin and they'd go off into the bush together.

In truth this reflects Beryl's own wishes and foreshadows her later actions, not those of Alice.

The two characters who consistently show the most insight into others are Linda Burnell and Jonathan Trout, brother- and sister-in-law; and it is only in the scene between them that fundamental issues are allowed to surface and to be tested and explored verbally. In the opening stages of their encounter each perceives with sympathy something of the other's human individuality and limitation of character. Jonathan observes Linda in her garden 'walking on again, with her little air of remoteness'. Linda watches Jonathan as he lies back on the grass and thinks: 'How attractive he was . . . What was the matter with Jonathan? He had no ambition; she supposed that was it. And yet one felt he was gifted, exceptional.' As their talk continues the two repeatedly confirm each other in their diagnoses — Linda's '[She] knew that he would never change' is balanced by Jonathan's 'I'm old, I'm old' and his summing up, 'Weak . . . weak. No stamina. No anchor. No guiding principle, let us call it,' echoing the symbolism of the early morning bathe. Their conversation is rambling, but circular, and in this sense whole, unlike the disjointed and linear conversations between the other characters, including Linda and Stanley.

The juxtaposition of scenes in 'At the Bay' is also thematically significant, as in *Prelude* and 'The Daughters of the Late Colonel'. The same metaphoric structure of analogy and contrast is present, as, for example, in the juxtaposition of the scene between Linda and Jonathan discussed above and the meeting of Linda and Stanley which immediately follows. Here the contrast emphasises the inadequacies of the relationship between Linda and Stanley, who do not communicate closely either on a verbal or non-verbal level. The relationship is more distanced than in *Prelude*, the misunderstandings more radical because more easily accepted.

Other key episodes run in parallel: for example, Beryl's encounter with Mrs Kember on the beach (Section V) and the later one with Harry Kember, who is a kind of double of his wife. More delicate still is the interplay between scenes such as that where Linda regards her baby son, and the one which follows in which Kezia begins to question her grandmother about the death of her Uncle William. These two episodes cannot be said to be either parallelled or contrasted; rather they interlock, and the themes of birth and death, youth and age are interwoven in a common light of acceptance.

Though it belongs to a different story cycle, 'At the Bay' is closely related in underlying theme to 'The Garden-Party'. Both stories seek, largely through the harmony which they themselves create, to overcome a deeply divisive sense of conflict and discord. The effort to 'see through' discontinuity is one which author and reader (and the characters) undertake alike in these stories.

'A Married Man's Story' belongs to the same month as 'At the Bay' and interrupted its composition. The *Journal* shows that on 8 August Katherine Mansfield was writing 'At the Bay'. A letter from Murry to Sydney Schiff[4] notes that on 23 August she was in the middle of the story then called 'A Married Man' and intended for the title story of her new collection. The story was set aside because of illness and not published until after her death. Though unfinished, it has strong claims on our attention as one of her most radical and experimental fictions.

Katherine Mansfield herself recognised the newness of the story, and the risks this newness entailed; she wrote of it, 'I am at present embedded in a terrific story but it still frightens me.' The quality of the story lies in its special use of first-person narrative, in an extension of the technique of 'Je ne parle pas français'. Like Raoul Duquette, the narrator of 'A Married Man's Story' is a literary man, and like Duquette he repeatedly draws our attention during the course of the story to his own activity in writing it:

> To live like this . . . I write those words very carefully, very beautifully. For some reason I feel inclined to sign them, or to write underneath — Trying a New Pen.

The story thus has a dual subject, the unfolding of the experience of the narrator, which gradually shades into a study of the means by which experience is conveyed in language (Katherine Mansfield neatly captured this ambiguity in writing of Raoul Duquette in 'Je ne parle pas francais' that he was 'the subject — I mean *lui qui parle*').

From very early on, the narrator of 'A Married Man's Story' plays with his sense of the means of expression open to him. He wants to tell 'everything, everything' — but how? A series of images, of rain falling all over the world, of an arrival in a strange city and of a departure by boat, of deserted gardens and a deserted road, is rapidly sketched in only to be as rapidly abandoned in favour of the image of 'a mournful glorious voice' which 'begins to sing in my bosom'. The first set of images is condemned as unsatisfactory by the narrator because they leave only 'the traces of my feeling'. The voice image is better, perhaps: 'Yes, perhaps that is nearer what I mean.'

Initially, as the narrator plays in this way with style and expression, we have the feeling that he is not much more than another Raoul Duquette. Like Duquette, he is given to self-dramatisation and has an acute sense of potentially good roles:

> It tempts me — it tempts me terribly. Scene: The supper-table. My wife has just handed me my tea. I stir it, lift the spoon, idly chase and then carefully capture a speck of tea-leaf, and having brought it ashore, I murmur, quite gently, 'How long shall we continue to live — like — this?' And immediately there is that famous 'blinding flash and deafening roar . . .'

However, as the story continues we learn that the narrator's self-awareness and hence the dual theme of the story is more complex. The metaphor of acting and play-acting continues, as in 'Je ne parle pas français' but is here counterpointed by a more urgent sense of the necessary artifice involved in any creative activity. As the narrator realises, even the most direct and simple of feelings cannot be expressed with simplicity, or naïveté: they require careful and patient manipulation of the forms of expression.

> That about the wolves won't do. Curious! Before I wrote it down, while it was still in my head I was delighted with it. It seemed to express, and more, to suggest, just what I wanted to say. But written, I can smell the falseness immediately . . . Tell me! Tell me! Why is it so difficult to write simply — and not simply also but *sotto voce*, if you know what I mean?

That is how I long to write. No fine effects — no bravura. But just the plain truth, as only a liar can tell it.

The point is made in a more direct way in the story, as the narrator-as-a-young-boy watches a girl in real distress coming into his father's shop for his famous fivepenny 'pick-me-up':

Suddenly the bell jangled and a young woman rushed in, crying so loud, sobbing so hard, *that it didn't sound real* [Our italics].

Art sounds more like life than life. Once the artist/writer becomes aware of this he will be poised continually on the knife-edge between 'truthfulness' of impression and the danger of slickness or falsity — precisely the problem which Katherine Mansfield felt she was facing, judging from her *Journal* comments on successful and unsuccessful stories.

The relationship between narrator and reader is one of the most unusual features of the story. In this text, as in 'The Canary', the writer seems to reach a point at which the 'speech' of the narrator (written or spoken) breaks reading conventions by not merely involving us in the experience described but explicitly demanding our complicity in its creation. This effect is produced by a variety of stylistic manoeuvres, for example the consistent use of the present tense to place us in close relationship with the narrator at the opening of each scene:

Do you remember your childhood? I am always coming across those marvellous accounts by writers who declare that they remember 'everything'. I certainly don't. The dark stretches, the blanks, are much bigger than the bright glimpses. I seem to have spent much of my time like a plant in a cupboard. Now and again, when the sun shone, a careless hand thrust me out onto the window-sill . . .

— and so back into the past. As we voyage backwards, the narrator continually turns to address the reader directly — 'Devilish! Wasn't it?', 'Am I being obscure? Well, the thing itself isn't so frightfully crystal clear is it?', and so on. A good deal of the pleasure of reading the story comes from the sense of shock generated by these appeals. We are not used to being addressed so summarily and directly in fiction: we are unused, as it were, to the text's need of us. 'A Married Man's Story' is not a self-confident and self-contained text, like a novel by George Eliot, for example. It constitutes instead a continual appeal to the reader. In 'Je ne parle pas français' and 'Poison' Katherine Mansfield questioned the relationship between experience and language. Here she questions the concept of experience itself as a valid external touchstone or point of reference for reader and writer. There can be no guarantee that they share the same world: on these grounds as well as linguistic ones the communicability of experience cannot be assumed or assured. This underlying solipsism (which is perhaps what 'frightened' her most about the story) is beautifully imaged in the boy's game with the candle:

> The night after, I lighted the candle and sat down at the table instead. By and by, as the flame steadied, there was a small lake of liquid wax, surrounded by a white, smooth wall. I took a pin and made little holes in this wall and then sealed them up faster than the wax could escape.

It is also expressed through the narrator's character as we see it unfold through the story. His experiences, which have made him what he is, are revealed gradually. We see him at the beginning of the story in a state of disengagement, coolly analysing the nature of the bonds which tie him.

> Why? Ah, there you have me! There is the most difficult question of all to answer. Why do people stay together? Putting aside 'for the sake of the children', and 'the habit of years' and 'economic reasons' as lawyer's nonsense — it's not much more — if one really does try to find out why it is that people don't leave each other, one discovers a mystery . . .

He goes on to tell us that he has not always been in this state of suspension and disengagement: that he and his wife were an 'ideal couple' before something that happened 'last autumn' — though we may doubt this information when we consider an incident recounted from early in the marriage. On the afternoon of their wedding day his wife asked him whether he thought physical beauty was 'so very important':

> I don't like to think how often she had rehearsed that question. And do you know what I answered? At that moment, as if at my command, there came a great gush of hard, bright sound from the band, and I managed to shout above it cheerfully, 'I didn't hear what you said.' Devilish!

During the course of the story the narrator is driven 'back and back' into the past to seek the causes of his present state. Unlike Raoul Duquette he accepts fully that the past influences the present, is indeed part of the present. He announces as his 'creed' his belief that 'Nothing Happens Suddenly'. In accordance with this belief the story shapes itself as a quest following the clues left by memory. As we watch, the memories form themselves into a significant pattern of images.

The narrator has been perverted as a child, not physically, but mentally and emotionally. His childhood is evoked through a series of surrealistically distorted pictures. His father's chemist's shop takes on the feverish vividness of a dream-image:

> I peered through to watch my father padding softly up and down. There were coloured windows on the landings. As he came up, first his bald head was scarlet, then it was yellow. How frightened I was! And when they put me to bed, it was to dream that we were living inside one of my father's big coloured bottles.

The colours of red and gold are repeated in the design of posters which he remembers on a wall opposite the shop. The wall suggests imprisonment, the posters hint at perverse sexual relationships:

I stand beside her, and we gaze at the slim lady in a red dress hitting a dark gentleman over the head with her parasol, or at the tiger peering through the jungle while the clown, close by, balances a bottle on his nose, or at a little golden-haired girl sitting on the knee of an old black man in a broad cotton hat . . .

The theme of sexual corruption is continued in the description of the 'gaudy' young women with their 'free ways' who come to his father for his pick-me-up. Their appearance is fantastic, and so, to the boy's perception, is his father's:

My father . . . Curled up in the corner on the lid of a round box that held sponges, I stared at my father so long, it's as though his image, cut off at the waist by the counter, has remained solid in my memory. Perfectly bald, polished head, shaped like a thin egg, creased, creamy cheeks, little bags under the eyes, large pale ears like handles.

This image shifts after the most disturbing scene in the story, when the boy's mother comes to tell him that his father has poisoned her. 'Was it a dream?' asks the narrator. It does not really signify, for whether literally or figuratively the father has poisoned his wife, who, mysteriously, has never recovered from childbirth. From this point on, the boy thus sees his father as 'awfully like a bottle, with his face for the label — *Deadly Poison*'.

The distortions which take place in the child's mind have a chilling inevitability in the light of his childhood environment in the alchemical den of the chemist's shop. The glowing lights of his father's glass jars, and the mysterious contents of his father's pick-me-up, both have the power to transform reality; and the shop itself, despite its dubious status, thus becomes a place of refuge. The shop is removed from reality and the frightening world of pain and suffering outside. Quite early on, the boy begins to follow the pattern of his father, withdrawing into the security of indifference and a refusal to be moved by the emotions of others. Even when a trick is played on him at

school and he finds a dead bird in his pocket, he remains
unmoved:

> How tightly the beak was shut! I could not see the mark where
> it was divided. I stretched out one wing and touched the soft,
> secret down underneath; I tried to make the claws curl round
> my little finger. But I didn't feel sorry for it — no! I
> wondered.

Yet the boy is also imaged as a young plant, capable of growth,
though only occasionally and randomly thrust out into the 'sun'
of possibility. The form which his growth takes is one of the most
intriguing aspects of the story.[5] Having formed no satisfactory
relationship with his parents or any other human beings, yet
sensing within himself unfulfilled emotional possibilities, the
child feels weighted down by an intolerable sense of dreariness:

> But while I played with the candle and smiled and broke off
> the tiny white peaks of wax that rose above the wall and
> floated them upon my lake, a feeling of awful dreariness
> fastened on me — yes, that's the word.

A strange 'flowering of the self' enables him to break out of this
prison through a mystical identification with the external world.
This mysticism satisfies his need for self-expression while at the
same time absolving him from human contact and responsibilities:

> And one big, bright green star I chose for my own. My star!
> But I never thought of it beckoning to me or twinkling merrily
> for my sake. Cruel, indifferent, splendid — it burned in the
> airy night. No matter — it was mine!

The perversity of this development is suggested through the key
image of the wolves: the boy is unnatural in seeking communion
only with the non-human world:

> You know those stories of little children who are suckled by
> wolves and accepted by the tribe, and how for ever after they
> move freely among their fleet, grey brothers? Something like

that has happened to me . . . I did not consciously turn away from the world of human beings; I had never known it; but I from that night did beyond words consciously turn towards my silent brothers . . .

The story ends here. It is clear that the narrator has never done more than pretend to normal human emotions and that some inner core of sympathy and responsiveness is lacking in him. His wife and child will never have the comfort which they look for from him, and it seems certain that he is specifically repeating the pattern of his parents' marriage in rejecting the child who came 'last autumn'. But the narrator is tormented by his knowledge. Although he senses that there may be an almost masochistic element in his wife which led her to seek him out, his logical mind will not let him get away with his actions on those grounds. Unlike Raoul Duquette, he has a conscience which is more than a superficial acquaintance with the forms of right and wrong. It is in the notion of conscience that the two themes of the story meet. For the narrator's conscience functions both as a guarantee of his greater interest as a character than, for example, Raoul Duquette, and points towards the greater linguistic sensitivity and delicacy which we may expect from his story. As an exploration of solipsism in both thematic and formal terms it is a story which in a sense fittingly has no ending. Murry was right in this case to call the story 'unfinished yet somehow complete'.

The Burnells of 'At the Bay' and 'The Doll's House' are an extended family group who appear mostly in domestic situations. Kezia is small and just beginning to open her eyes on the possibilities of the world which the adults, Linda and Beryl especially, foreshadow in their own problems. All the Burnell stories are about discovery and the growth of that kind of awareness which belongs with the intense, singular perspective of the small child. For the later stage of growth, the stage of adolescent self-consciousness and its social adjustments, Katherine Mansfield invented another family, the Sheridans.

Like the Burnells, the Sheridans are a Wellington family who live in Tinakori Road, the place from which in *Prelude* we see the Burnells moving to live in Karori. There is no grandmother and no small child in the Sheridan family, only the two parents with three adolescent girls and a younger boy. Katherine Mansfield had spent the years from five to ten in Karori, and moved back to Tinakori Road where she was born, in 1898, to a new house, much larger than her birthplace, the house displayed with some precision in 'The Garden-Party'.

She had more difficulty with the Sheridan stories than the Burnell stories. They lacked the impetus of the *Karori* concept, the idea of knitting all the Burnell stories into a discontinuous but cohesive novel. The process of discovery which is basic to both cycles was more straightforward in the Burnell group, since the focus was on objects or incidents seen as isolated phenomena in the present moment of the child's wide-eyed perspective. The Sheridan stories are more concerned with human relationships, the impact of local conditions on the developing personality and how the present affects the past and future. In a letter written in March 1922 Katherine Mansfield described the Sheridan preoccupations as 'the diversity of life and how we try to fit in everything, Death included'.[6] The Burnell stories deal with involuntary change and development, while the Sheridan stories are concerned with conscious change.

Partly as a result of this difficulty she completed little of the projected Sheridan cycle. Ian Gordon includes sixteen pieces, dated between 1915 and 1922, in the Sheridan stories printed in *Undiscovered Country*, including 'Maata' and 'The Wind Blows'.[7] But only the last five seem to have been designed specifically as a Sheridan cycle. A fragment called 'A Dance' which appears in the *Journal*, tentatively dated 1920,[8] was reconstructed as the first Sheridan story, 'Her First Ball', in July 1921. 'By Moonlight', which was never finished, was written in September 1921, and the only major Sheridan story, 'The Garden-Party', in October 1921. A further piece, called 'The Sheridans', was begun in May 1922 probably with the idea of developing the stories into a complete cycle on the *Karori* model for publication in *The Sphere*. Nothing else was set down, however, before she gave up writing altogether.

Of this group only 'The Garden-Party' is a masterpiece. There was no pillar to provide underpinning of the kind that *Prelude* gave to the Burnell cycle. Katherine Mansfield wrote in the manuscript of 'Her First Ball' that it was only playing on the borders of the sea (the sea of adolescent discovery),[9] and a month later she wrote of 'By Moonlight', giving as her reason for abandoning it that 'This isn't bad, but at the same time it's not good. It's too easy.'[10] So to take up the Sheridan family again for 'The Garden-Party' was a risk and a challenge.

It was a challenge partly because the subject, an adolescent encounter with death, demanded a more orthodox narrative structure than 'At the Bay' or 'The Daughters of the Late Colonel'. The 'Garden-Party' is told as a single character's story in a straightforwardly sequential narrative. It is not divided into scenes or sections or 'cells'[11] and Laura, the central figure, is the consciousness through which everything is observed throughout the day's events. This tighter unity was necessary because the story is more narrowly than the Burnell stories an account of adolescent discovery, and of Laura's recognition, through confrontation with death, of the distance which is beginning to develop between her and her family.

The development of Laura's differences from her family is shown in a number of ways. Her growth as an adolescent is implied, for instance, in the affinity she feels for the men of the story as much as it is shown by her divergence from her mother and sisters. Her father and her brother both respond to the news of the death down the lane more sympathetically and therefore more as Laura does than any of the female Sheridans. Laura feels a precise affinity with her brother at the end of the story, the same kind of affinity that she tells herself she feels for the workmen in her garden at the beginning. The dead man's widow and sister-in-law make little impression on her, for all their swollen faces, compared with the peaceful sleep of the dead man. Laura's world is beginning to stretch beyond the narrowly feminine confines of family and garden.

At the outset of the story her distance from her mother and sisters is only a matter of inclination. She is sent to tell the workmen where to erect the marquee because 'you're the artistic one'. In the middle, when news of the death down the lane is first delivered, the fact that she reacts in the opposite way to her sister and her mother is linked to her sense of comradeship with her brother.

> When the Sheridans were little they were forbidden to set foot [down the lane] because of the revolting language and of what they might catch. But since they were grown up, Laura and Laurie on their prowls sometimes walked through. It was disgusting and sordid. They came out with a shudder. But still one must go everywhere; one must see everything. So through they went.

Near the end, after Laura's first impulse to stop the party because of the death has been diverted by her mother's diplomacy, and the party has gone its delightful course, Laura is drawn into her mother's belated impulse to send a basket of party left-overs to the dead man's family, but now feels much more distinctly alone.

> Again, how curious, she seemed to be different from them all. To take scraps from their party. Would the poor woman really like that?

Her journey down the dark lane among the dark people with the incongruous relic of the day is an adventure she takes on her own, out of her family's protection. It is her first real voyage of discovery. It is an encounter with a world which has been hitherto a male preserve, where knowledge of death is a necessary part of reality.

Mrs Sheridan will have nothing to do with such adventures. Although she uses the party as a ritual of initiation into adulthood for her children ('I'm determined to leave everything to you children this year'), her vision of the adult world does not extend beyond the garden.

> 'Mother, a man's been killed,' began Laura.
> '*Not* in the garden?' interrupted her mother.
> 'No, no!'

'Oh, what a fright you gave me!' Mrs Sheridan sighed with relief, and took off the big hat and held it on her knees.

She is an adroitly diplomatic stage-manager, allowing her children to think they are in complete control of the party, redirecting Laura by means of the beautiful hat into what she sees as the normal channel of adolescent conduct, with enough success to ensure that Laura is standing 'side by side' with her on the porch to farewell the guests after the party has ended. Only the male reminder of the death down the lane, what Mrs Sheridan feels to be her husband's distinctly tactless remark, renews her distance from her daughter. She is the perfect mother for childhood and the sheltered butterfly life of the Sheridan house and garden. Laura's divergence from her signals a departure from childhood.

The distance is also marked by that feature of the story which has troubled so many commentators, the element of social class. New Zealand critics tend to feel it is overstated, a British intrusion on their classless society. Other critics feel it is over-stated because the contrast with the elegiac beauties of the garden party inside the Sheridan gates is melodramatised. Both kinds of objection put too high a priority on external realism and see the social setting in terms of its independent existence, not in relation to Laura and her growth which is the focus for the whole story.

Laura herself of course calls the social element 'these absurd class distinctions', and refuses to recognise them. To her mother they are second nature. She does not like having to deal with the lower classes. Laura is sent in her place to negotiate with the workmen over the placing of the marquee, Jose is sent to be diplomatic with the cook, and Laura is dispatched with the basket to the dead carter's family. Mrs Sheridan keeps her distance from workmen just as she enjoins her children to keep away from their cottages in the dark lane. But Laura ventures among the workmen just as she had ventured with her brother among the cottages. She rejects her mother's aversion because 'one must go everywhere'. She feels initially a warmth for the workmen with the marquee in an unconsciously patronising manner which is only a small shift away from her mother's aloofness. She is in a different world from them.

> 'H'm, going to have a band, are you?' said another of the workmen. He was pale. He had a haggard look as his dark eyes scanned the tennis-court. What was he thinking?
>
> 'Only a very small band,' said Laura gently. Perhaps he wouldn't mind so much if the band was quite small.

The dark eyes do not belong with bands and parties and all the attendant brightness.

Laura's sister Jose is more like her mother: 'Jose loved giving orders to the servants, and they loved obeying her. She always made them feel they were taking part in some drama.' But Laura, the artistic one, has begun her journey in a different direction.

> Oh, how extraordinarily nice workmen were, she thought. Why couldn't she have workmen for friends rather than the silly boys she danced with and who came to Sunday night supper? She would get on much better with men like these.

It is a direction which culminates in her visit to the dead carter, a visit which measures not only her distance from her family but the leap she has been forced to make from her own childish assumptions about nice workmen.

This kind of measurement is the basic feature of the story and the prime reason for its more orthodox narrative structure. Laura makes a single journey through the events of the day in sequence, concluding with the real journey she goes on out of her garden and down the dark lane. The structure follows that sequence in time and with the cohesion of the single viewpoint. It is a mildly comic paradox that this sequential structure should have produced the chief complaints about the story, its disunity.[12] The contrast between the glorious perfections of the party and the misery of the dead man's home has produced several protests about the violence of the disjunction. And yet the whole story is built on it. The transition from bright morning to dark evening and the related patterns of contrast are the essential accompaniments to Laura's process of discovery.

The contrasts are numerous and exact. The transition of time from the morning's discoveries through the afternoon party to the evening's discoveries is gradual, but the details at either end form a pattern of sharp contrasts. The Sheridans' garden, with its roses, its lily-lawn, its tennis-court and the grove of karaka trees, contrasts with the cottages.

> They were little mean dwellings painted a chocolate brown. In the garden patches there was nothing but cabbage stalks, sick hens and tomato cans.

The cream puffs bought for the garden party appear before and after. Before, they are sampled with guilty delight by Laura and Jose; after, they are scraps loaded into the basket for the poor: 'All those sandwiches, cakes, puffs, all uneaten, all going to be wasted.' And lilies, the pink cannas which are delivered on the morning of the party like the cream puffs, and the arum lilies, the white funeral flower, which are only withdrawn from the gift of leftovers because they would stain Laura's frock, likewise appear before and after.[13] Cream puffs and lilies are first delivered to the bright Sheridan property by the workers, the baker's man and the florist, and then are delivered by Laura to the dark property of the workers as leftovers. The 'blaze' of canna lilies and the bright cream puffs, together with all the main images of light, the morning, the colourful garden, are transmuted into images of dark, the 'deep shade' of the lane, the 'dark knot' of people at the garden gate where the dead body is housed, the 'gloom' of the cottage and in the end Laurie stepping out of the shadows. In the first part of the story people are all coming into the light, entering the glories of the Sheridan garden bringing gifts for the party. In the second half Laura goes out of the brightness on an antithetical journey carrying gifts from the party into the darkness of the lane.

Two images in particular stand out in this pattern of contrasts, and link the imagery explicitly with the central subject, the encounter with death. The beautiful hat with which Mrs Sheridan distracts Laura's mind before the party, is black, a 'black hat trimmed with gold daisies, and a long black velvet ribbon'. Like the lilies, it makes a dazzling show for the party, but like the white arum lilies which Mrs Sheridan wants Laura to take down the lane it is also a version of the trappings conventionally taken to funerals. Laura does not recognise it as such. The hat belongs with the party, and therefore is an embarrassment when she hurries down the lane with the basket of cream puffs.

How her frock shone! And the big hat with the velvet streamer — if only it was another hat!

Finally she is taken to view the body. Dazed by its stillness she is forced to apologise to it for her misconceived symbol.

There lay a young man, fast asleep — sleeping so soundly, so deeply, that he was far, far away from them both. Oh, so remote, so peaceful. He was dreaming. Never wake him up again. His head was sunk in the pillow, his eyes were closed; they were blind under the closed eyelids. He was given up to his dream. What did garden parties and baskets and lace frocks matter to him? He was far from all those things. He was wonderful, beautiful. While they were laughing and while the band was playing, this marvel had come to the lane. Happy . . . happy . . . All is well, said that sleeping face. This is just as it should be. I am content.

But all the same you had to cry, and she couldn't go out of the room without saying something to him. Laura gave a loud childish sob.

'Forgive my hat,' she said.

The hat is her cream puff, the relic of gaiety she carries with her from the party. When she had shut the gates of the Sheridan garden behind her, she was filled with the party: 'It seemed to her that kisses, voices, tinkling spoons, laughter, the smell of crushed grass were somehow inside her.' Now it is outside her, incongruously shining on her head, the device intended to shine in the very process of giving her shade from the brightness. And for this display of childish pleasures she must now apologise.

The other and even more direct contrast linking the party with death is Jose's song.

Pom! Ta-ta-ta *Tee*-ta! The piano burst out so passionately that Jose's face changed. She clasped her hands. She looked mournfully and enigmatically at her mother and Laura as they came in.

This Life is *Wee*-ary,
A Tear — a Sigh.
A Love that *Chan*-ges,
    This Life is *Wee*-ary,
A Tear — a Sigh.
A Love that *Chan*-ges,
And then . . . Good-bye!

But at the word 'Goodbye', and although the piano sounded more desperate than ever, her face broke into a brilliant, dreadfully unsympathetic smile.

'Aren't I in good voice, mummy?' she beamed.

This Life is *Wee*-ary,
Hope comes to Die.
A Dream — a *Wa*-kening.

In the middle of the preparations for the party the song seems merely ludicrous. The reality, with its explicit echo in Laura's reaction to the sight of the body ('He was dreaming. Never wake him up again'), is a contrast which measures Laura's advance in awareness over Jose, while at the same time marking her desperate romanticising of the corpse. She views the body as if she were in a fairy tale. The dead carter is a sleeping prince whom she has braved many terrors to reach. And when she sees him she sees his stillness as a peaceful sleep from which he must never be awoken. Instead of the sleeping princess to be roused with a kiss there is a sleeping prince to be left in peace. He is happy. All is well. He suffers none of the pains of life and parties and incongruous hats. So she can return from the darkness with the bright image from its centre, the magical awakening hers alone, and her magical brother's.

Laurie put his arm round her shoulder. 'Don't cry,' he said in his warm, loving voice. 'Was it awful?'

'No,' sobbed Laura. 'It was simply marvellous. But, Laurie

—' she stopped, she looked at her brother. 'Isn't life,' she stammered, 'isn't life —' But what life was she couldn't explain. No matter. He quite understood.

'*Isn't* it, darling?' said Laurie.

And there the story ends. It is a cycle of growth. The roses open their petals for the morning of the party; the afternoon 'slowly ripened, slowly faded, slowly its petals closed'. At the end the corpse lies like a closed flower in the night, and Laura feels she has seen life through its full cycle of blossoming and closure.

Laura's learning process in the course of the day is radical, though it is also far from complete. The ending, the inexpressible discovery about life, marks her encounter with the fact of death rather than her assimilation of its full significance. The positiveness she voices to Laurie at the conclusion is in its immature confidence, and the assurance that Laurie '*quite* understood', a signal of the distances her journey still has to cover. Death is still more melodramatic to her than real. Her sleeping prince is marvellous because he reveals the completion of the cycle of life blossoming rather than the finality of death as a denial of life. Some such thought may have been in Katherine Mansfield's own mind when she wrote at the end of her manuscript, 'This is a moderately successful story, and that's all. It's somehow, in the episode at the lane, scamped.' Life is stronger in 'The Garden-Party' than death. Those critics who approve it for its elegiac evocation of the beautiful life shy away from the dark side of the pattern of contrasts and from the transition between light and dark. But since Laura does not leave the Sheridan property for the lane until more than four-fifths of the way through the story they can claim some support for their view, both in the space given to the one over the other, and in the author's own verdict.

It is, however, a quantitative assertion which underrates the central function of Laura herself, and the gradual nature of the process which takes her away from the world of Mrs Sheridan's values. Laura is a chrysalis — Jose has already emerged as a butterfly like her mother ('Jose, the butterfly, always came down in a silk petticoat and a kimono jacket' — and the story rests on the brief intrusion of death into the butterfly world. Laura's own emergence is only beginning. The garden party is a growth point, and it is rightly portrayed as a brilliant, idyllic setting for the incipient butterfly. The final emphasis on Laura's emergence from her protective cocoon cannot cancel the idyllic glories of the butterfly world of the Sheridan garden. But the butterfly garden is also incomplete without the recognition that it can hatch creatures possessing a greater sense of engagement with life than the butterflies.

'The Doll's House' is a Burnell story set at Chesney Wold in Karori, when Kezia is rather older than in *Prelude* and attending school with her older sisters. It was completed on 30 October 1921, and appeared as the first story in *The Doves' Nest*, the volume which was in preparation when Katherine Mansfield died and which came out posthumously in 1923. It thus matches *Prelude*, which opened *Bliss, and Other Stories*, and 'At the Bay', which was the first story in *The Garden-Party, and Other Stories*. The Burnell world set the tone for all three of the major collections.

In a *Journal* note for 27 October 1921, under the heading 'Stories For My New Book', 'The Doll's House' is entered under its original title: 'At Karori', the name given it when it was first published in *The Nation* for 4 February 1922. The note read:

> N.Z. *At Karori*. The little lamp. I seen it. And then they were silent.[14]

This was presumably the author's reminder to herself of the story's conclusion, and its key, which stands in the published text as:

> Presently our Else nudged up close to her sister. But now she had forgotten the cross lady. She put out a finger and stroked her sister's quill; she smiled her rare smile.
>
> 'I seen the little lamp,' she said softly.
>
> Then both were silent once more.

The sun, which symbolises so much in Katherine Mansfield's fiction, took on a new shape and a new focus as the symbolic lamp of the last of the Burnell stories.

Although 'The Doll's House' is a return to the Burnell family, it carries with it from 'The Garden-Party' strong elements of class consciousness, almost as if it was an extension of the Sheridan story, an elaboration of the background to Laura's journey. Socially the Karori school is heterogeneous, and the mix is nearly complete.

> . . . all the children of the neighbourhood, the Judge's little girls, the doctor's daughters, the store-keeper's children, the milkman's, were forced to mix together. Not to speak of there being an equal number of rude, rough little boys as well. But the line had to be drawn somewhere. It was drawn at the Kelveys. Many of the children, including the Burnells, were not allowed even to speak to them. They walked past the Kelveys with their heads in the air, and as they set the fashion in all matters of behaviour, the Kelveys were shunned by everybody.

The parental voice is heard here, affirming parental selection of the ritual scapegoats. Social outcasts have to exist as a reassurance that lines can be drawn and held. The attitude is Mrs Sheridan's, and the story is one of Kezia's resistance against her mother's values in a form which stresses her affinity with Laura Sheridan.

The parental voice is heard throughout the story, though Mrs Burnell herself only appears as a momentary voice when she forbids Kezia to cross the line drawn against the Kelveys.

> 'Mother,' said Kezia, 'can't I ask the Kelveys just once?'
> 'Certainly not, Kezia.'
> 'But why not?'
> 'Run away, Kezia; you know quite well why not.'

The parental attitude is pervasive because it is mimicked by the children. Emmie Cole 'nodded to Isabel as she'd seen her mother do on those occasions'. The children share the parental need to identify the outsiders and hold them away from the area of privilege. The Kelvey children also adopt parental attitudes; Lil when ordered away by Aunt Beryl is seen 'huddling along like her mother'. These are crude imitations, but they imitate the bluntness of the parents. ' "Your ma told our ma you wasn't to speak to us," ' says Lil Kelvey to Kezia. The Kelvey children accept the line just as readily as the children above it, and presumably as readily as their mother, who is described in a mixture of authorial and parental voices as

> a spry, hard-working little washerwoman, who went about from house to house by the day. This was awful enough. But where was Mr Kelvey? Nobody knew for certain. But everybody said he was in prison. So they were the daughters of a washerwoman and a gaolbird. Very nice company for other people's children!

Only Kezia, the smallest in her family's pecking order, takes no part in the general pecking at the Kelveys. She is a princess in the Burnell royal family, and accepts alongside her sisters the homage paid to their treasure, the doll's house, in the Burnell 'courtyard'. But she would like to extend the social right of homage even to the Kelveys, and that wish plants the seed of her own alienation.

As outsiders the Kelvey children appear through animal images. When they stand on the edge of the circle of children in the school playground, Else Kelvey is 'a little white owl', silent, still, with enormous solemn eyes. When Kezia breaks through the social line by inviting them into the courtyard to see the treasure they move 'like two little stray cats'. When Beryl asserts the pecking order she shoos them away 'as if they were chickens'. Like animals they squeeze through the white gate of the courtyard, while Beryl thinks of them as 'those little rats of Kelveys'. Everyone in the story is little, except for Mrs Burnell's disembodied voice, but the Kelveys are smaller in their appearance as small animals than anyone else.

Kezia herself is neither cat, rat nor chicken. She is the youngest Burnell, heir like her sisters to the family treasure and willingly fitting into the family hierarchy.

'I'm to tell,' said Isabel, 'because I'm the eldest. And you two can join in after. But I'm to tell first.'

There was nothing to answer. Isabel was bossy, but she was always right, and Lottie and Kezia knew too well the powers that went with being eldest. They brushed through the thick buttercups at the road edge and said nothing.

'And I'm to choose who's to come and see it first. Mother said I might.'

The hierarchy, like the line drawn against the Kelveys, is an extension of parental rule. Kezia has no conscious thought of rebelling against it.

The Kelveys first show themselves in Kezia's consciousness only as a routine presence on the edge of the circle of courtiers surrounding the Burnells. Nothing leads up to her question about inviting them which brings Mrs Burnell's sharp refusal. It precedes the point when, everyone having seen the doll's house except the two Kelveys, their exclusion from the court emphasises their scapegoat status. But when it has been emphasised in this way, and when the long shadows of the Kelveys reach the white Burnell gate, Kezia makes her decision to break the circle and challenge the hierarchy.

Now she could see that they were the Kelveys. Kezia stopped swinging. She slipped off the gate as if she was going to run away. Then she hesitated. The Kelveys came nearer, and beside them walked their shadows, very long, stretching right across the road with their heads in the buttercups. Kezia clambered back on the gate; she had made up her mind; she swung out.

Kezia is swinging, balanced on the edge of decision. She does not really calculate ('She slipped off the gate as if she was going to run away', not a positive action). Only the large shadows of the little Kelveys force her into choosing independent action. They stretch like a barrier right across the road.

Kezia's introduction of the Kelveys into the courtyard is cut short by angry Beryl, tormented by her own private challenge to cross over not the social but the sexual line: 'A letter had come from Willie Brent, a terrifying, threatening letter, saying that if she did not meet him that evening in Pulman's Bush, he'd come to the front door and ask the reason why!' In her anger Beryl breaks off the Kezia—Kelvey link and Kezia disappears from the story. She goes before anything beyond the tentative act of juvenile patronage can develop. For all her transgressing of the parental lines, she is primarily creating her own act of homage, matching her elder sister with her processions of little girls coming respectfully two by two in order to view the treasure. Only one detail, the little lamp, suggests a larger perspective.

To Kezia the lamp is the prize exhibit in the doll's house. The others value the toy versions of adult possessions, but the lamp is art.

And Isabel's voice, so very proud, went on telling. The carpet made a great sensation, but so did the beds with real bed-clothes, and the stove with an oven door.

When she finished Kezia broke in. 'You've forgotten the lamp, Isabel.'

'Oh yes,' said Isabel, 'and there's a teeny little lamp, all made of yellow glass, with a white globe that stands on the dining-room table. You couldn't tell it from a real one.'

'The lamp's best of all,' cried Kezia. She thought Isabel wasn't making half enough of the little lamp. But nobody paid any attention. Isabel was choosing the two who were to come back with them that afternoon and see it. She chose Emmie Cole and Lena Logan. But when the others knew they were all to have a chance, they couldn't be nice enough to Isabel. One by one they put their arms round Isabel's waist and walked her off. They had something to whisper to her, a secret. 'Isabel's *my* friend.'

Only the little Kelveys moved away forgotten; there was nothing more for them to hear.

Isabel queens it over the playground. Nobody inside the circle hears Kezia's special plea for the lamp. But outside the circle clustered round Isabel there are the other two listeners. They hear Kezia, and at the end of the story Else shows that the point registered. The lamp sits at the heart of the treasure, and the Kelveys were brought to it by Kezia. Else and Kezia, the youngest sisters, share the same values. The lamp, symbol of light and in its toy form symbol of childish awakening, is the central reality.

> But what Kezia liked more than anything, what she liked frightfully, was the lamp. It stood in the middle of the dining-room table, an exquisite little amber lamp with a white globe. It was even filled all ready for lighting, though, of course, you couldn't light it. But there was something inside that looked like oil and moved when you shook it.
>
> The father and mother dolls, who sprawled very stiff as though they had fainted in the drawing-room, and their two little children asleep upstairs were really too big for the doll's house. They didn't look as though they belonged. But the lamp was perfect. It seemed to smile at Kezia, to say, 'I live here.' The lamp was real.

In this, the last major story in the Burnell and the Sheridan groupings of stories, Katherine Mansfield returns to her longest-lasting concern, art, and to her most rewarding technique, symbolism. The little lamp is not only light but art, the central reality amidst the material splendours of the doll's house. It shines out to Kezia and reaches across the gulf between the young Burnell princess and owlish little Else. It stands as a symbol against all the materialist values of the stiffly sprawling parents, seen by the few, but a reward all the more intense for its inaccessibility and the rarity with which it is achieved.

'The Fly' was written in February 1922, while Katherine Mansfield was undergoing X-ray treatment in Paris. It was a story which she 'hated writing', though it is one which has produced a wealth of critical commentary, most notably in a series of articles in *Essays in Criticism* in 1962 and *The Explicator* rather earlier, in the 1940s. The *Essays in Criticism* series began with an article by F. W. Bateson and B. Shahevitch in which they argued that in

'The Fly' Katherine Mansfield employed the techniques of narrative realism, using 'irrelevant descriptive detail' in order to make the external setting of the story seem 'historically authentic', thus causing the reader to suspend his disbelief and enter the world of the story. Examples of 'irrelevant detail' which they cited were the *green* chair on which Mr Woodifield sits (why Mr Woodifield?), and the minute description of the son's photograph.

In a reply, E. B. Greenwood refined on this idea in pointing out that such use of detail could not always be called 'irrelevant'. It might often function metonymically, as the boss's furniture does, standing in part for its owner and exhibiting some of his characteristics, in this case his materialism and love of display.

Later commentators on 'The Fly' have concentrated more on the metaphysical implications of the story and its allegorical or symbolic aspects. Interpretations here have differed widely: the boss has been seen as a god-like figure; alternatively he has been called a fellow human for whom we feel sympathy as he encounters grief for the first time; or he is represented as a coarse and brutal representative of the generation which unthinkingly sent its sons to war.

There seem to be two main problems in criticism of 'The Fly'. First, despite the numerous analyses of the story, the theoretical insights of critics like Greenwood have not been pursued or developed. So it is necessary at this point to affirm once again the complexity of Katherine Mansfield's fictional technique. As in all her stories, detail in 'The Fly' almost invariably functions on both narrative and symbolic levels. Thus the description of the boss's furniture, which Bateson categorised as 'irrelevant' and Greenwood saw as metonymic, also works as part of the total symbolic structure of the story. The much debated 'greenness' of Woodifield's chair is in keeping with the natural and pastoral aspects of his character, which are set in opposition to the city-bound, mechanical qualities of the boss. The description of the son's photograph is also crucial for thematic development, for it images, as in 'The Daughters of the Late Colonel' and 'At the Bay', 'mechanical' memory or memory by rote, which has long replaced natural memory or grief in the boss.

In 'The Fly' the demands of symbolist patterning are crucial in shaping the distinctive form and texture of the narrative. Katherine Mansfield's method is essentially the same from 'The Wind Blows' and *The Aloe* through to her last story, 'The Canary'. But despite the inherent complexity of its method, 'The Fly' seems finally to lack the fullness and richness of implication of her finest work. This might be called the second 'problem' for criticism. The story has attracted so much critical attention that it is assumed to be virtually her best work. It could however be argued that it is precisely because the story is flawed that it has provoked so many conflicting interpretations.

The flaw seems to lie in the rigidity of the story's shaping idea. Primarily it invites us to make a metaphysical equation between the boss as he toys with the life of the fly, and God or the gods, playing with the lives of human beings 'for their sport'. The author would have expected us to have Gloucester's dictum in mind as we read, and even without this allusion we could hardly fail to appreciate the pointed juxtaposition of the three deaths in the story — that of the fly and those of the boss's and Woodifield's young sons. However, in the context of the story, the equation has a simplicity which verges on the crude. For it is not, as it is in *King Lear*, a moving but momentary interpretation of man's plight. The idea dominates the story and is not substantially modified or qualified by other events and images. Thus we miss in 'The Fly' the rich suggestiveness which we find in other stories with a similar theme: for example, 'The Garden Party', with its shifting perspectives and changes of tone. The conflicting roles of the boss as both man and god, which have inspired so much comment, are a direct consequence of the idea's dominance over suggestive detail. The symbol of the fly is too inflexible for the developing purposes of the story.

In a sense 'The Fly' is too consciously created, the product of what Katherine Mansfield herself called her regrettable tendency to 'cleverness'. If this impression is correct, then 'The Fly' can be related to other stories which she was writing at this time for *The Sphere*. Hard pressed for money to pay for her medical treatment, she wrote to Ida Baker of the necessary relation between 'work' and 'wealth' during this period in Paris. The stories written for *The Sphere* (for example, 'Honeymoon' and 'Taking the Veil') reflect in differing degrees the strain of writing to market requirements and deadlines. However, in pointing to this element in 'The Fly' one is not saying that it is a weak story, as some she wrote for *The Sphere* indubitably are. It is on the contrary a very powerful one, and some of its images are hauntingly suggestive, as, for example, the chilling parallel between the spectral park of the boy's photograph, and the park-like cemetery in which he now lies:

> But he did not draw old Woodifield's attention to the photo-graph over the table of a grave-looking boy in uniform standing in one of those spectral photographers' parks with photographers' storm-clouds behind him. It was not new. It had been there for over six years. . . .
> 'There's miles of it,' quavered old Woodifield, 'and it's all as neat as a garden. Flowers growing on all the graves. Nice broad paths.' It was plain from his voice how much he liked a nice broad path.

It seems necessary to draw attention to the flaws in the story in order to correct a critical imbalance. Fortunately, there is an early precedent for critical reserve about it. When Katherine Mansfield wrote that she 'hated' writing it, she was replying to a letter from William Gerhardi in which he told her of his dislike of the story. She responded characteristically;

> I am sorry that you did not like *The Fly* and glad that you told me.

Katherine Mansfield's development of indirect free form was one of her most important contributions to the art of the short story. Such a form allowed for directness and immediacy, enabling the intrusive presence of the author-as-narrator to *appear* to disappear from the text. We have already seen an example of the technique in the opening of 'Bliss', and there are numerous further examples: for example, this from 'Miss Brill':

Miss Brill put up her hand and touched her fur. Dear little thing! It was nice to feel it again. She had taken it out of its box that afternoon, shaken out the moth-powder, given it a good brush, and rubbed the life back into the dim little eyes. 'What has been happening to me?' said the sad little eyes. Oh, how sweet it was to see them snap at her again from the red eiderdown!

In her first-person narratives Katherine Mansfield went further in freeing the story from the presence of the author-narrator figure. These first-person narratives are at the opposite pole from those of the conventional short story, in which the 'I', the teller of the tale, is divorced from the action and functions as a witness or commentator. In Mansfield's first-person narratives, it becomes increasingly hard to distinguish an author-narrator separable from the central character-as-narrator — we have seen something of this progression in following the development from 'Je ne parle pas francais' to 'A Married Man's Story'.

'The Canary' (completed 7 July 1922) differs from the other first-person narratives in that it is presented entirely as spoken monologue. For this reason it moves even further outside normal narrative conventions. Not only is the author-narrator figure invisible, but the audience, in the conventional sense, also disappears. For in most narrative forms, including the diary-confessional mode of 'Je ne parle pas' and 'A Married Man's Story', there is a convention of the reading audience providing a role into which the reader slips unthinkingly. In direct transcription of speech, the form adopted for 'The Canary', there is no easy position for the reader to take up in the text. He is placed in the position of overhearing speech not intended for him (because not written), yet not intended for any other audience identified for him in the text (which would make the text into a story within a story). The reader is therefore drawn into the text to form its only possible audience and to complete the circle of its creation. This accounts for the immediacy of effect, combined with the fact that the speaker's confession mimics the breach of convention which we feel in 'real life' when someone transgresses normal social boundaries to make unforeseen revelations or confessions.

The meaning of 'The Canary' largely resides, as in all the stories, in symbolism and purposeful organisation of the text. The canary is a symbol of the artist, as is evident from the story itself, without reference to the many uses of the image in letters and journals. The canary is described in this way:

> . . . You cannot imagine how wonderfully he sang. It was not like the singing of other canaries. And that isn't just my fancy. Often, from the window, I used to see people stop at the gate to listen, or they would lean over the fence by the mock-orange for quite a long time — carried away . . .

Within the framework of this story about a canary, the real artist explores some of the deepest themes of her work. The story is, of course, elegiac. It opens with the theme of mortality, and remembrance:

> . . . You see that big nail to the right of the front door? I can scarcely look at it even now and yet I could not bear to take it out. I should like to think it was there always even after my time. I sometimes hear the next people saying 'There must have been a cage hanging from there.' And it comforts me; I feel he is not quite forgotten.

The elderly woman goes on to talk of the artistry of the canary's song, and of the human need for beauty, a need which is related to some inadequacy, some felt flaw in human life:

> . . . Then I loved the evening star . . . It seemed to understand this . . . something which is like longing, and yet it is not longing. Or regret — it is more like regret.

The emptiness of the woman's life and the pain she has suffered from the limited contacts which she has had with other human beings are conveyed largely through description of a 'cruel' and 'dreadful' dream which only the canary could help her to control and subdue. As the story draws to its close, the solitary speaker asserts the uniqueness of the canary — she will never have another bird. This one can never be replaced. By implication, the uniqueness of the artist is also affirmed, and we remember

Katherine Mansfield's belief in the intense individuality which is at the root of the artistic personality.

A sense of normality is then tentatively established as the woman confirms that she will, of course, get over the death of the canary. She will, that is, accommodate herself to knowledge of death and a forced awareness of the transitoriness of beauty.

Up to this point, the monologue has proceeded in a relatively disjointed manner. Each paragraph begins with an ellipsis and the effect is of a speaker gradually collecting her thoughts. Yet the speech is cumulative, and is directed. Everything leads up to the final paragraph, in which the author, within the symbolic context of the story, makes a statement about her own art, expressing in dramatic form what it is she wishes to convey beneath, or through, her 'joyful song':

> . . . All the same, without being morbid, and giving way to — to memories and so on, I must confess that there does seem to me something sad in life. It is hard to say what it is. I don't mean the sorrow that we all know, like illness and poverty and death. No, it is something different. It is there, deep down, deep down, part of one, like one's breathing. However hard I work and tire myself, I have only to stop to know it is there, waiting. I often wonder if everyone feels the same. One can never know. But isn't it extraordinary that under his sweet, joyful little singing it was just this — sadness? — Ah, what is it? — that I heard.

In this final speech punctuation and cadence are adjusted with perfect finesse to achieve an effect of poetic intensity while retaining the comparatively simple vocabulary of the woman speaker. The triumph of this final paragraph is also a triumph over the solipsism explored in 'A Married Man's Story'. Here, the author paradoxically *expresses* her sense of the isolation of human beings in a formal context which almost literally *forces* communication between reader and writer. In the absence of an identifiable audience in the story we as readers must fill this vacancy, and thus we are placed virtually in the same relationship to the speaker as in 'real life'. So when she says that she 'often wonders if everyone feels the same' we are in a position where we have to respond, to accept and test the premise offered. We cannot dismiss it in the same way in which we can dismiss the distanced utterance of a third person 'character' in a different kind of fiction in which many alternative perspectives are available.

'The Canary' had its genesis in a single image which Katherine Mansfield returned to throughout her career, from her 1915 reference to herself as an artist, 'so bound, so *caged*, that I know I'll *sing*', to a letter written just a few months before the story:

> The woman in the room opposite has a wicker cage full of canaries. How can one possibly express in words the beauty of their quick little song rising, as it were, out of the very stones . . . And there sits the woman in her cage peering into theirs . . . It is very strange.[15]

The symbolism of 'The Canary' has a reach and depth which seem to go hand-in-hand with the technical inventiveness and exploratory quality of the story. Katherine Mansfield wrote in a review of 1919,

> There is a title which the amateur novelist shares (but how differently!) with the true artist: it is that of experimentalist. However deep the knowledge a writer has of his characters, however finely he may convey that knowledge to us, it is only when he passes beyond it, when he begins to break new ground, to discover for himself, to experiment, that we are enthralled. The 'false' writer begins as an experimentalist; the true artist ends as one.[16]

It is appropriate that her last story should enthrall us in exactly this way, embodying the artist's own high ideals.

Notes

Chapter 1

[1] *Adam*, no. 300 (1965). Ida Baker was persuaded to give these recollections, quoted in Miron Grindea's editorial, pp.4-5.

[2] *Katherine Mansfield's Letters to John Middleton Murry 1913-22*, ed. J. Middleton Murry (London, Constable 1951), p.149 (1 February 1918).

[3] See, for example, *Ibid.*, p.290 (8 June 1918).

[4] Leonard Woolf, *Beginning Again, An Autobiography of the Years 1911-18* (London, Hogarth Press 1964), p.204.

[5] Christopher Hassall, *A Biography of Edward Marsh* (London, Longmans 1959), p.226.

[6] *The Journal of Katherine Mansfield*, 'Definitive Edition' (London, Constable 1954), p.275 (December 1921).

[7] *Between Two Worlds: An Autobiography* (London, Cape 1935), pp. 433-4.

[8] *Daniel Deronda*, Penguin edn. p.694.

[9] *Journal*, pp. 93-4.

[10] *The Country of the Blind, and Other Stories* (London, Nelson 1911), pp.iv-v.

[11] *Novels and Novelists, by Katherine Mansfield*, ed. J. Middleton Murry (London 1930), p.32.

[12] *The Letters of Katherine Mansfield*, ed. J. Middleton Murry, 2 vols. (London, Constable 1928), II, 145 (October 1921).

[13] *Journal*, pp.313-14.

[14] In her early notebooks K.M. made extensive notes on two of Symons's books, *Studies in Prose and Verse* (London, Dent 1904) and *Plays, Acting and Music* (London, Constable 1909). She probably read others of his books as well.

[15] *Journal*, p.273.

[16] *Letters*, II, 88 (17 January 1921).

[17] See Bibliography for a select checklist of published criticism.

Chapter 2

[1] Alexander Turnbull Library: Mansfield MS Papers, Acc. 97285, Notebook 40.

[2] The use of long phrases or clauses in parallel construction, sometimes with similar sounds in similar places in the parallel phrases or clauses.

[3] *The Native Companion*, p.131.

4 See Ruth Mantz and J. M. Murry, *The Life of K.M.* (London, Constable 1933), p.269.

5 Wrongly listed as a poem in Sylvia Berkman, *Katherine Mansfield: A Critical Study* (New Haven, Yale UP 1951), p.213.

6 It was Roman Jakobson who first pointed out, in a famous paper — 'Two Aspects of Language and Two Types of Aphasic Disturbances' — that in general poetic and Symbolist writing tends to proceed according to perceptions of similarity (or contrast), rather than according to perceptions of contiguity, as in realistic narrative. See *Fundamentals of Language*, ed. Jakobson and Halle (The Hague, Mouton 1956). This is a regular feature of K.M.'s work and of other Symbolist prose writers.

7 *The Collected Stories of Katherine Mansfield* (London, Constable 1945), p.524. Since the stories are for the most part brief, and numerous editions are now available, subsequent references will be by story rather than by page.

8 This is the first appearance of the hat image which is used so powerfully in 'The Garden Party' to suggest worldly temptation.

9 In a very early piece, 'My Potplants' (?1903), K.M. borrowed the format of *Elizabeth and her German Garden*. She obviously knew her cousin's work well.

10 *The Black Monk and other Stories* (London, Duckworth edn. 1903), p.187.

11 Proceeding according to perceptions of contiguity, that is, proximity in place or time.

12 Musical term for a theme associated throughout a piece with a person, situation or sentiment.

13 E.g. Berkman, p.49.

14 Both uncollected. 'A Marriage', *New Age* (7 March 1912); 'Gwendolen', *New Age* (2 November 1911), first attributed to K.M. by J. Garlington, 'An Unattributed Story by K.M.?', *MLN* LXXI (1956), pp.91-3.

15 *The New Age* (7 March 1912), pp.449-50.

16 Hulme used — or distorted — Bergsonian ideas to lend support to his attacks on post-Renaissance Humanism, attacks originally inspired by the philosophy of Wörringer. His philosophy is often associated with that of Wyndham Lewis, also a contributor to *The New Age*.

17 *Letters*, II, 165 (19 December 1921).

18 'Spatial Form in Modern Literature', *Sewanee Review* LIII (1945), pp.221-40, 433-56, 643-53.

19 *Rhythm*, II, 13 (1913), p.426.

20 Anthony Alpers, *Katherine Mansfield* (London, Cape 1954), p. 153, writes that K.M. had first send Murry a 'fairy story', which puzzled him. He asked her to send something else and 'after a little delay' she replied with 'The Woman', which fitted in admirably with *Rhythm*'s slogan, misquoted from Synge, 'Before art can be human again it must learn to be brutal'.

21 Ian A. Gordon, *Undiscovered Country* (London, Longman 1974), p.xviii.

22 *Letters*, II, 92 (3 February 1921, to R. Murry).

23 *Journal*, p.205. The entry (made in April 1920) is headed 'The Flowering of the Self'.
24 Nigel Nicholson and Joanne Trautmann (eds.), *The Question of Things Happening: The Letters of Virginia Woolf Vol. 2, 1912-1922* (London, Hogarth Press 1976), p.262.
25 T. S. Eliot used this famous phrase to denote an external symbol or correlate for a private emotion.
26 Murry dates *The Aloe* (as published by him in 1930) in 1916, i.e. written largely during the time of his and K.M.'s 'idyll' in Bandol. C. K. Stead, in 'Katherine Mansfield and the Art of Fiction' *The New Review* 4, 42 (September 1977), pp.27-36 has however suggested that this draft was composed essentially in 1915. He cites evidence to point to her having spent only about two weeks on *The Aloe* in Bandol.
27 *Journal*, p.205.

Chapter 3

1   *Letters to J.M.M.*, p.114 (11 January 1918).
2   *Ibid.*, p.51 (12 December 1915).
3   *Ibid.*, p.344 (20 October 1919).
4   'Nietsche contra Wagner', in *The Case of Wagner*, trans. A. M. Ludovici ed. Oscar Levy (London, T. N. Foulis 1911), pp.77-8.
5   *Letters to J.M.M.*, p.566 (18 October 1920).
6   *Letters*, II, 196 (13 March 1922).
7   Eliot discussed three short stories: 'Bliss', Lawrence's 'The Shadow in the Rose Garden', and Joyce's 'The Dead'.
8   Letter to Virginia Woolf (undated), *Adam*, 370, p.19.
9   Elizabeth Bowen, for example, in her introduction to a selection of K.M.'s work (see Bibliography pp.140, 142). Margaret Drabble has also discussed the element of 'cruelty' in 'The New Woman of the Twenties: Fifty Years On', *Harpers and Queen* (June 1973), pp.106-7, 135.
10 *The Diaries of Virginia Woolf*, ed. Anne Olivier Bell (London, Hogarth Press, 1977), I, 179.
11 *Letters to J.M.M.*, p.211.
12 *Between Two Worlds*, p.463.
13 *Journal*, p.192.
14 *Letters to J.M.M.,* pp.400-1 (21 November 1919).
15 *Ibid.*, p.194 (3 March 1918).
16 *Ibid.*, p.454.
17 Quoted by F. A. Lea, *The Life of John Middleton Murry* (London, Methuen 1959), p.77.
18 *Letters to J.M.M.*, p.598 (21 November 1920).
19 *Ibid.*, p.393 (16 November 1919).
20 *Letters*, II, 88-9 (17 January 1921).
21 *Letters to J.M.M.*, pp.604-5 (end November 1920).

[22] Functioning ironically, for the lily is normally associated with virginal whiteness and purity.

[23] *Collected Stories*, p.523.

[24] *Katherine Mansfield: The Memories of L.M.* (London, Michael Joseph 1971), p. 153.

[25]

[26] *Ibid.*, II, 87 (1 January 1921).

[27] For a more detailed study of the symbolic images, see Don W. Kleine, 'Mansfield and the Orphans of Time', *Modern Fiction Studies* 24 (1978-79), pp.428-38.

[28] *Letters*, II, 120 (23 June 1921).

[29] *New Literary Values* (Edinburgh, Oliver and Boyd 1936), p.105.

Chapter 4

[1] It was completed 14 August. *Journal,* p.259.

[2] K.M. had read her Bergson years before Virginia Woolf, and the opposition in his philosophy of 'clock time' and 'real time' is equally strong in her work.

[3] *Letters to J.M.M.*, p.577 (30 October 1920: letter on *The Autobiography of Margot Asquith*).

[4] BM MS 52921.

[5] Compare in this context K.M.'s condemnation of Murry's mystical tendencies, e.g. in her famous comment that he couldn't fry a sausage without thinking of God.

[6] *Letters*, II, 196.

[7] *Undiscovered Country*, 'Summer'.

[8] *Journal*, pp.209-10.

[9] *Journal*, p.258.

[10] *Ibid.*, p.262.

[11] *Undiscovered Country*, p.xix.

[12] A point first made by Warren S. Walker in 'The Unresolved Conflict in "The Garden Party" ', *MFS* 3 (1957-58), pp.354-8.

[13] *Canna hybrida* is a bright red lily-like subtropical flower. *Zantedeschia aethiopica*, the arum lily, is a large white flower with a prominent yellow spadix in the centre. It was a standard form of funeral decoration, and more generally signified purity.

[14] *Journal*, p.268.

[15] Letter to 'Elizabeth' (21 February 1922; BM MS 50844).

[16] *Novels and Novelists*, p.119.

Bibliography

(Place of publication London, unless otherwise stated)

Collected Works

Collected Stories (Constable 1945).

The Complete Stories of Katherine Mansfield, (Auckland, Golden Press 1978). Contains 'Brave Love', the story first published in *Landfall* 1972 (see below).

Selected Stories, chosen and introduced by D. M. Davin, World's Classics edn. (1953), and subsequent Oxford University Press paperback edns.

Thirty-Four Short Stories by Katherine Mansfield, selected and introduced by Elizabeth Bowen (Collins 1957).

Undiscovered Country: The New Zealand Stories of Katherine Mansfield, ed. I. A. Gordon (Longman 1974).

Separate Works

In a German Pension (Stephen Swift 1911), reprinted by Penguin Books.

Prelude (1918), hand-printed at the Hogarth Press.

Je ne parle pas français (1918), privately printed.

Bliss, and Other Stories (Constable, 1920), reprinted by Penguin Books.

The Garden-Party, and Other Stories (Constable 1922), reprinted by Penguin Books.

The Doves' Nest, and Other Stories (Constable 1923).

Something Childish, and Other Stories (Constable 1924: published in the United States by Knopf as *The Little Girl*).

Poems (Constable 1923).

The Aloe (Constable 1930).

Novels and Novelists (Constable 1930).

    Contains all the reviews of fiction K.M. contributed to *The Athenaeum* 1919-20.

New Material

Most of K.M.'s letters and notebooks are held by the Alexander Turnbull Library, Wellington, N.Z. The following additional material has been culled from their holdings:

Juliet (K.M.'s early, unfinished novel), *Turnbull Library Record*, Wellington, N.Z. (March 1970).

Maata (substantial amounts of her second novel, also unfinished), *Turnbull Library Record* (May 1974, May 1979).

'Brave Love' (a complete story dating from 1915), *Landfall* (1972).

The Urewera Notebook, ed. I. A. Gordon (Oxford University Press 1978). A transcript of the notebook K.M. kept while on her 1907 camping trip. Only fragments have been published previously.

Autobiography

Journal, ed. J. Middleton Murry (Constable 1927). A further 'Definitive Edition' was published in 1954, but see articles by I. A. Gordon and P. Waldron, below, for Murry's handling of K.M.'s journal/notebook material.

The Letters of Katherine Mansfield, ed. J. Middleton Murry, 2 vols. (Constable 1928).

The Scrapbook of Katherine Mansfield, ed. J. Middleton Murry (Constable 1939).

Katherine Mansfield's Letters to John Middleton Murry, 1913-22, ed. J. Middleton Murry (Constable 1951).

The Letters and Journals of Katherine Mansfield, A Selection, ed. C. K. Stead (Penguin 1977).

Note: An edition of K.M.'s collected letters is being prepared by Margaret Scott for Oxford University Press, London. An edition of John Middleton Murry's letters to her is also planned, based on the Turnbull Library holdings.

Biography

Mantz, R. E., and Murry, J. M., *The Life of Katherine Mansfield* (Constable 1933). This deals only with K.M.'s early years, and has some inaccuracies.

Alpers, A., *Katherine Mansfield: A Biography* (Cape 1954).

Alpers, A., *The Life of Katherine Mansfield* (Cape 1980). The revised edition contains much new material.

Katherine Mansfield: The Memories of L.M. (Michael Joseph 1971).

Carswell, J., *Lives and Letters: A. R. Orage, Beatrice Hastings, Katherine Mansfield, John Middleton Murry, S. S. Kotelianshy, 1906-1957* (Faber 1978). Interesting background material for the *New Age* period of K.M.'s career.

Meyers, J., *Katherine Mansfield: A Biography* (Hamish Hamilton 1978). Again new material, but tends to be over-speculative in some sections.

Critical Works

Berkman, S., *Katherine Mansfield: A Critical Study* (New Haven, Yale University Press 1951). Relates K.M.'s work and her life.

Gordon, I. A., *Katherine Mansfield*, Writers and their Work (Longman 1954; revised edition 1971).

Daly, S. R. *Katherine Mansfield* (Twayne English Authors Series, New York 1965).

Magalaner, M., *The Fiction of Katherine Mansfield* (Southern Illinois University Press 1971).

Articles

Adam International Review 300, 370 (1965, 1972).
  Both issues contain articles on K.M. and previously unpublished letters: issue 370 is devoted entirely to K.M.

Aiken, C., 'The Short Story as Poetry' in *Collected Criticism* (Oxford University Press 1968), pp.291-9.

Alcock, P., 'An Aloe in the Garden: Something Essentially New Zealand in Miss Mansfield', *Journal of Commonwealth Literature (JCL)* XII, 3 (April 1977), pp. 58-64.

Bateson, F. W., and Shahevitch, B. 'Katherine Mansfield's "The Fly": A Critical Exercise', *Essays in Criticism* 12, 1 (1962), pp.39-53. Replies to this articles appear in subsequent issues in the same volume.

Bowen, E., 'Introduction' to *Thirty-Four Short Stories* (Collins 1957).

Brophy, B., 'Katherine Mansfield', *London Magazine* 2, 9 (December 1962), pp.41-7.

Davis, R. M., 'The Unity of the Garden Party', *Studies in Short Fiction* II (1964), pp.61-5.

Drabble M., 'The New Woman of the Twenties: Fifty Years On', *Harpers and Queen* (June 1973), pp.106-7, 135.

Eliot, T. S., in *After Strange Gods* (Faber and Faber 1934).
  'Bliss' is discussed pp.35-6.

Garlington, J., 'Katherine Mansfield: The Critical Trend', *Twentieth Century Literature* II, 2 (1956), pp. 51-61.
  A useful survey of critical opinion up to the fifties.

Gordon, I. A., 'The Editing of Katherine Mansfield's *Journal* and *Scrapbook*', *Landfall* 13, 1 (March 1959), pp.62-9.

Hankin, C., 'Fantasy and the Sense of an Ending in the Work of Katherine Mansfield', *Modern Fiction Studies (MFS)* 24, 3 (1978-79), pp.465-74.

Hynes, S., 'Katherine Mansfield: The Defeat of the Personal', *South Atlantic Quarterly* 52 (1953), pp.555-60.

Justus, J., 'Katherine Mansfield: The Triumph of Egoism', *Mosaic* VI, 3 (1973), pp.13-22.

King, R. S., 'Katherine Mansfield as an Expatriate Writer', *JCL* VIII, 1 (1973), pp.97-109.

Kleine, D., 'The Chekhovian Source of "Marriage à la Mode" ', *Philological Quarterly* 42 (1963), pp.284-8.

Kleine, D., 'Mansfield and the Orphans of Time', *MFS* 24, 3 (1978-79), pp.428-38.

Magalaner, M., 'Traces of her "Self" in Katherine Mansfield's "Bliss" ', *MFS* 24, 3 (1978-79), pp.413-22.

Meyers, J., 'D. H. Lawrence, Katherine Mansfield and *Women in Love'*, *London Magazine* 18, 2 (May 1978) pp.32-54.

Modern Fiction Studies 24, 3, (1978-79).
This special Katherine Mansfield issue contains articles by D. W. Kleine, C. Hankin and M. Magalaner, among others.

Mortelier, C., 'Origine et Développement d'une Légende: Katherine Mansfield en France', *Etudes Anglaises* XXV, 4 (1970) pp.357-68.

Nebeker, H., 'The Pear Tree: Sexual Implications in Katherine Mansfield's "Bliss" ', *MFS* 18 (1972-73), pp.545-51.

O'Sullivan, V., 'The Magnetic Chain: Notes and Approaches to K.M.', *Landfall* 114 (June 1975), pp.95-131.

Pritchett, V. S., 'Review of *Collected Stories'*, *New Statesman* (2 February 1946).

Stead, C. K., 'Katherine Mansfield and the Art of Fiction', *The New Review*, 4, 42 (September 1977), pp.27-36.

Taylor, D. S., and Weiss, D. A., 'Crashing "The Garden Party" ', *MFS* 4, 4 (1958), pp.361-4.

Waldron, P., 'Katherine Mansfield's *Journal'*, *Twentieth Century Literature* XX, 1 (January 1974), pp.11-18.

Walker, W.S., 'The Unresolved Conflict in "The Garden Party" ', *MFS* 3, (1957-58), pp.354-8.

Walsh, W., *The Manifold Voice* (Chatto and Windus 1970), a study of Commonwealth literature, has a chapter on K.M. pp.154-84.

Bibliography

There is no adequate bibliography for K.M. Ruth Mantz's 1931 *The Critical Bibliography of Katherine Mansfield* (Constable) contains many errors, some of which have been corrected in S. Berkman's *Critical Study* (see above).

Index